WHAT DOES THE LORD REQUIRE?

* * *

WHAT DOES THE LORD REQUIRE?

THE OLD TESTAMENT CALL TO SOCIAL WITNESS

* * *

BRUCE C. BIRCH

The Westminster Press
Philadelphia

Book design by Gene Harris

First edition

Published by The Westminster Press®
Philadelphia, Pennsylvania

PRINTED IN THE UNITED STATES OF AMERICA

2   4   6   8   9   7   5   3   1

Library of Congress Cataloging in Publication Data

Birch, Bruce C.
  What does the Lord require?

  Bibliography: p.
  1. Sociology, Biblical. 2. Bible. O.T.—Theology.
3. Church and social problems. I. Title.
BS1199.S6B57 1985   261.1   85-610
ISBN 0-664-24630-3 (pbk.)

What does the Lord require of you
but to do justice, and to love kindness,
and to walk humbly with your God?

Micah 6:8

*   *   *

CONTENTS

*   *   *

PREFACE

M any church members and pastors will readily admit
that the Old Testament is a problem to them. They
find it difficult to read and understand. Its world seems
remote and alien. Unfortunately, the help available to
them has been of a limited character. Adult education
materials in the local congregation have tended to stress
knowledge of our ancient historical background in Old
Testament times without communicating the importance of those witnesses for our contemporary faith.
Many pastors tell of seminary courses where the emphasis was entirely on a critical understanding of the history
and literature of the Old Testament, with little or no
attention given to Old Testament theology. The practical result of this situation has been to relegate the Old
Testament to second-class status as scripture, with few
people regarding its witness as central to their faith.

This situation has begun to change. In the last two
decades there has been a steady recovery of interest in the
Old Testament and the importance of its witness to the
modern living of the Christian faith. There are several
factors contributing to this recovery. The translation
into English of the great Old Testament theologies of
Gerhard von Rad and Walther Eichrodt in the early
1960s began a steady stream of exciting publications in

the area of Old Testament theology. These now extend
from technical scholarly works to works intended for use
in the local congregation. The widespread use of the
lectionary for preaching and teaching has encouraged
pastors to tackle Old Testament texts more often, thus
giving their congregations greater exposure to the Old
Testament witness. In educational settings ranging from
theological seminaries to lay study events, Old Testament subjects are receiving renewed attention.

It is hoped that this small volume will contribute further to such a recovery. It is intended for study and use
in the local congregation, and in fact it originated out of
the study experience of a congregation of urban Christians called the Sojourner Community. Sojourners is a
community of evangelical Christians living in the inner
city of Washington, D.C., who believe that their faith
commitment requires their faithful response and witness
to the pressing issues of our time. This responsive witness has ranged from activity in behalf of peace to spon-
sorship of day care and housing for the inner-city poor.
They are perhaps most widely known for the publication
Sojourners, a monthly magazine of witness from a Christian perspective on the most serious issues facing the life
of the church and the world.

In the fall of 1982, Sojourners asked me to do a series
of week-night sessions with the community as a part of
their regular study and worship life together. We chose
to do an overview of the Old Testament themes that are
still central to our faith, and it was a rich time together.
At the end of those weeks Jim Wallis, the editor of the
magazine, asked if I might be interested in writing a
series for the magazine similar to the study sessions we
had just completed. He felt that many of the magazine's
readers undervalued the Old Testament as a faith re-

source and that such a series would help broaden the biblical base of the magazine's witness.

The series began in the January 1984 issue of *Sojourners* under the title "What Does the Lord Require?" taken from the verse in Micah 6:8. It appeared in six parts (roughly every other month), concluding in December of 1984. Some of the material was adapted from *The Predicament of the Prosperous* by Bruce C. Birch and Larry L. Rasmussen (Westminster Press, 1978) and my chapter "The Covenant at Sinai: Response to God's Freedom" in *Social Themes of the Christian Year* ed. by Dieter T. Hessel (Geneva Press, 1983). The Westminster Press has now agreed to bring the Sojourners articles out in book form in order to make them available to a wider audience. To aid in this use, study questions and suggestions for further reading for each chapter have been added at the back of the book. But the chapters have not been rewritten from the material submitted for the magazine series, and thus they are of necessity limited in scope.

This book is *not* a survey introduction to the Old Testament. There are important parts of the story of Israel and the witness of its traditions that are given only cursory mention or no treatment at all. Since the series was limited to six installments, some difficult choices had to be made on what to include and exclude.

This book is also *not* a critical scholarly analysis of Old Testament themes. There are no footnotes, although the suggestions for further reading include some of the resources that informed the writing of each chapter. Debates and disagreements over the interpretation of Old Testament themes and events have not been discussed here. Detailed analyses of individual books and texts have not been included. An attempt has been made to rely as much as possible on widely held understandings of the basic witness of central Old Testament traditions and to interpret those for a wider church audience. It is possible that future critical scholarship will alter some of the details, but it is unlikely that the broad outlines of the treatment here will be changed.

This book *is* an invitation to the Old Testament and its rich witness to the God of our faith. The stress is on Old Testament themes and understandings that are essential to Christians today. The hope in writing these chapters has been that many will discover Old Testament roots to their faith that they had not been aware of before. If this happens, it is hoped that many will go on to further study, filling in the gaps left by this limited treatment.

A special focus of this book is on the particular elements of the Old Testament tradition that inform the church's contemporary social witness. It is a special strength of Israel's faith that a division between spiritual and secular, personal and social dimensions of faith is simply not recognized. Inner faith commitment simply must find external expression in response to the concerns and challenges of the world. It has thus been a special hope for this study book that it might help provide a broader biblical base for a Christian faith characterized by deep inner commitment, on the part of persons and communities, and courageous ministry and witness to the needs of a broken world.

It is customary to end prefaces with acknowledgments, and I have only one. It is to Sojourners, the community and the magazine staff, with thanks for all the lives touched by their ministry, including my own.

I

In the Image
of God

*   *   *

M any of those in the churches who are most concerned for the witness of the Christian faith in the
social order find themselves hard pressed to describe a
significant role for the Bible in that task of social witness.
It is not that they do not honor the scripture, but that it
seems to become a kind of distant historical background
rather than a direct resource in addressing the urgent
needs of our broken world. A socially committed pastor
once said to me after I had spoken on biblical understandings of hunger issues, "That was interesting, but we
really don't have time to be reading the Bible. People are
starving out there."

One of the reasons for this is that Christian social
witness in our time has become chiefly identified with
the "doing" side of the Christian moral life. "What shall
we do about＿＿＿?" You can fill in any issue of concern:
peace, racism, poverty. The emphasis is on decision-mak-
ing, strategy, and action. Some of the church's finest
moments in our time have come when Christians made
decisions of conscience and courageously acted on those
decisions.

The Bible, however, does not make decisions for us or
plan courses of action. Attempts to use the Bible as a rule
book are not very successful. There are, of course, broad

moral imperatives, such as the command to love our neighbor, which are of central importance, but the church is left with the struggle to decide what the loving act toward the neighbor might be in a given situation. Many issues our society faces—nuclear war, environmental damage—were not anticipated at all by the biblical communities. Even when we share a common concern with those communities, such as feeding the hungry, we must make decisions and take actions in a complex global economic system totally unlike anything imagined in the biblical tradition.

Does this make the Bible remote or irrelevant to our Christian social concern? By no means! Alongside the concern for the ethics of "doing" lies an ethics of "being." Christian social concern requires not only that we ask what we should *do* in a broken world but also that we ask who we are to *be*. The shaping of the decision-makers is as important as the shaping of the decision. As we enter and are nurtured by the Christian community, we form values, perspectives, and perceptions that inform our deciding and acting. The identity we bring with us as Christians deeply affects our participation in ministering to a broken world.

In the shaping of our Christian "being," or identity, the Bible plays a central role. We encounter its witness in the preaching, teaching, and liturgy of the church, and we are shaped by it. Stories, hymns, histories, parables, and visions become as important as commandments and ethical teachings in molding the faith perspective through which we view our broken world and seek to mediate God's healing.

It is for this reason that those who are committed to the task of Christian social witness as a natural outgrowth of Christian faith must seek the broadest possible understanding of the biblical inheritance that is ours. To settle for a narrow acquaintance with our biblical traditions is to limit the faith vision we bring with us to the task of discerning God's will for a broken world. Unfortunately for many in the church, there is an entire portion of scripture that is inadequately known and poorly understood. Our use of its resources is highly selective and often pulled out of context. The portion of which I speak is the Old Testament.

The Old Testament as Scripture

It is not uncommon to run across persons in the church who declare that they are New Testament Christians. The implication is that they can do without the Old Testament entirely, or at best that the Old Testament has less authority than the New. This is a bit like trying to affirm only one person of the Trinity. In every period of its history and in all its major traditions, the church has refused to part with the Old Testament or to reduce its status as fully scripture. Both the Old Testament and the New are considered to be the Word of God, and since we believe in only one God the two portions of our scripture are linked by witness to a single divine reality. The Old Testament was quoted by Jesus and the apostles as scripture. To understand Jesus Christ as the center of our faith is not to reject the God of the Old Testament, but to see that same God acting out in Christ the final and fullest chapter in the great drama of God's salvation which began with the story of Israel.

Some of our attitude toward the Old Testament is caused simply by a lack of acquaintance with its contents, but we have also been the victims of some misconceptions.

Many believe that the church actually holds the Old Testament to be second-class scripture, or that the church has replaced the Old Testament with the New. Such views are actually versions of a position taken by Marcion in the second century A.D. He utterly rejected the Old Testament as authoritative and accepted only the Pauline epistles and the Gospel of Luke as authentic witness to our faith. He believed that the God of the Old Testament was a God of law who was different from the God of love revealed in Jesus Christ. The purpose of God in Christ was to overthrow the God of law (who was also the creator). Marcion's views were declared heretical and the early church opposed them, claiming the Old Testament to be a witness to the activity of the same God revealed to us fully in Jesus Christ; thus they declared both the Old Testament and the New to be the scripture of the church, the Word of God for God's people. This position was reaffirmed by the theologians of the early church, the Protestant Reformers, and the early preachers of the American religious movements and revivals. It is still the position of all major Christian traditions today.

Another misconception takes the form of stereotyping: the Old Testament is law while the New Testament is gospel. This is often meant to characterize the Old Testament as primarily judgment and the New as grace, but it does not do justice to the richness of either the Old or the New Testament. A picture of God's wrath and judgment can certainly be found in the Old Testament, and these pictures of God as warrior or judge are sometimes a problem for us. But the same side of God's nature can also be seen in the New Testament: in the book of Revelation, or in Jesus' cleansing of the temple, or in some of Jesus' harsh words to the Pharisees and others who oppose God's kingdom. On the other hand, the definitive picture of God's grace in Jesus Christ has already been preceded by a rich tapestry of witness to God's grace in the Old Testament: God's creation and blessing of the world, God's presence in history to bring Israel out of bondage in Egypt and to identify with all who suffer and are oppressed, God's call to become the covenant community, and God's forgiveness and comfort offered even to those whose sin takes them into exile. The law is, of course, an important Old Testament theme, but not as an end in itself. Unless law serves God's grace, we can find ourselves in bondage to the law, as the apostle Paul observed. However, when law follows grace it is not opposed to gospel, as Jesus himself proclaimed: "Think not that I have come to abolish the law and the prophets; I have come not to abolish them but to fulfil them" (Matt. 5:17).

It is the goal of this book to recover the Old Testament roots of our faith and to highlight the manner in which those roots inform the witness of the church in the modern social order. Spiritual and social dimensions of faith will interrelate in this series as they do in the Old Testament. The constant working assumption will be that the God revealed to us in Israel's story in the Old Testament is the same God who comes to us in Jesus Christ. We cannot fully understand who the New Testament proclaims Jesus to be unless we know the God who comes to us in Jesus as already revealed in the Old Testament story, from creation onward.

It is always difficult to choose a starting point when dealing with the Old Testament witness as a whole. Israel as a people come to birth in the events surrounding the deliverance out of Egypt recorded in the book of

Exodus. To start here would be to begin with God's salvation, and, indeed, most of our best materials on the Old Testament have stressed the salvation history of Israel, the mighty acts of God in moments of crisis. Only out of this awareness of its own salvation did Israel later begin to understand that God was also the Creator and giver of the promise to the ancestors in the stories of Israel's early traditions (Genesis). To begin with Israel's birth in Exodus would make sense.

We have chosen, however, to begin with the beginning not of Israel but of all beginnings; we speak first of creation. The whole of scripture starts with creation, and by passing on the tradition in this form the ancient biblical community must have intended us first to encounter the God who creates and then to read of the God who saves. It is true that the creation stories that open the book of Genesis received written form later in Israel's history, but we are not concerned here with literary development. We will begin with the picture of what God intended us to be in creation. When our faith story culminates in Jesus Christ, it is to return to a picture of what we are intended to be—new creation.

IN THE BEGINNING

The materials that witness to Israel's faith in God as Creator are scattered throughout the Old Testament. The Psalms, several of the Prophets (especially Deutero-Isaiah), and the Wisdom literature (e.g., Proverbs, Job) all contain rich and important creation passages. In the limited space available here, however, we will look primarily at the two creation accounts that open the book of Genesis. They touch on all major elements of the Old Testament witness to Creator and creation

The whole of scripture opens with the well-known creation story in Genesis 1:1–2:4a. This is the story that follows the formal, almost liturgical, seven-day pattern. In the beginning is a formless, watery chaos out of which God brings order by the mere command of divine word, " 'Let there be light'; and there was light" (Gen. 1:3). Creation begins with the great elements of the cosmos: light, waters, firmament, dry land. It then moves to the various life forms on the earth: plants, animals, and finally humanity itself. The seventh day is the day of God's rest, establishing the Sabbath as a memorial to God's creative work (cf. Ex. 20:8–11).

The creation story of Genesis 1 is immediately followed and in many ways balanced by the creation account in Genesis 2:4b–25. It is the human creature, created by God at the very beginning of the account, who occupies the center of attention throughout the story. Things do not seem to be created as separate orders; rather, humans, plants, and animals are all created for harmonious relationship. The Garden of Eden is the symbol of total and idyllic harmony. Even the earth itself is a part of this picture. Humanity is created from the dust of the ground. The Hebrew words themselves indicate closeness: *'adam* (humanity), *'adamah* (soil). In this account God is the creator, but not in the remote and sovereign sense of Genesis 1. God creates almost as a loving craftsman, intimately shaping the first human creature and breathing life into it. God then responds to the needs of this human creature in subsequent acts of creation. God is concerned for harmonious balance in this creation even to the point of dividing the first human creation into male and female to make the full relationship of sexual union and unity possible.

The God Who Creates and Blesses

Although these two creation stories are quite different in emphasis and details, they are marvelously complementary. This is especially clear in the pictures of God as Creator. Each account shows a different side of our faith understanding of God as Creator, and a lack of either would leave us with an impoverished and incomplete theology of creation.

In Genesis 1 the stress is on the absolute *sovereignty* of God. God's word alone calls the world into existence. Unlike the other ancient Near Eastern religions, God vanquishes no other primeval powers to create the world. In Babylonian mythology the god Marduk had to defeat the monster Tiamat in order to create. As a result, Babylonian religion lived constantly with the need to reenact that battle lest the order of creation fail. The Hebrews by contrast knew a God who is declared in Genesis 1 to be unrivaled, and who creates as an act of divine grace and freedom. Nothing compels the creation except God's own creative will. "The Lord by wisdom founded the earth; by understanding he established the heavens; by his knowledge the deeps broke forth, and the clouds drop down the dew" (Prov. 3:19–20). Confidence in the absolute sovereignty of God is reflected in a sense of the reliability of the creation which is God's work.

A picture of the Creator only in terms of divine sovereignty could leave us with a remote and transcendent God. Fortunately, Genesis 2:4b–9 balances the picture with a stress on the *relatedness* of God. Here God fashions the first creature like a loving craftsman, breathes the very breath of life into it, and relates caringly to the needs of this human creature. God walks and talks in the garden and is anguished when sin breaks the harmonious relationship (Genesis 3). In this story we come to know our Creator God as a caring, intimately related God, involved with the creation from the very beginning. It will not surprise us to find such a God involved once again in our redemption.

The combination of these two pictures of God the Creator points us to a unique dimension of the God of our faith. The sovereign yet related Creator foreshadows a constant biblical picture of a God whose power is expressed in vulnerability to the world's suffering, whose mysterious otherness comes close to us in intimate relationship. For those who know such a God, the exercise of power must always be tempered by caring relationship.

In these creation stories God not only creates, God also blesses. The verb itself appears in 1:28: "And God blessed them." The concept of a blessing from God appears in the constant divine concern for the well-being of the creation. God pronounces each element of the creation good (Genesis 1); God provides for the care of creation (Gen. 1:28–30 and 2:15), sees to the provision of needs (Gen. 2:9, 18), and continues to sustain all creatures, human and nonhuman ("These all look to thee," Ps. 104:27).

We know the God of blessing not only as the Creator who called the world into being but in the ongoing reliability of the created order and in the divine presence that sustains life in all its week-to-week rhythms. This aspect of God is present with us in all moments and is universally known by all humanity. God's intention in creation is for all to experience *shalom,* a Hebrew word meaning wholeness.

In the Old Testament, the God who creates and blesses helps to balance the tradition of a God who saves. The church in its use of the Bible has usually stressed the God who saves, for that is where we as a particular community of faith come into relationship to God. The mighty acts of salvation from Exodus to Resurrection stress the particular moments of crisis where we have known God's redeeming power. To acknowledge and serve this God who saves compels the church to respond in the midst of the crises of our time by bringing aid and hope, both spiritual and material.

But God is not found in the crises alone. God acts not only to deliver but to sustain us in all of life. To begin as we have with creation is to be reminded of God's relationship to all creation and not simply to our Judeo-Christian tradition. We are called not only to crisis intervention in a broken world but to the creation and maintenance of faithful systems of order that mediate the blessings of full life to all creation, persons and environment. To know God as Creator will force the church not only to interventions of the moment but to the building of *shalom.*

THE CREATION AND THE CREATURES

The opening chapters of Genesis reveal to us something of the Creator and speak also of the creation itself. It is here that we begin to discover what it means to be given life as a creature and to live that life in relationship to God and the rest of the created order.

One of the most important themes in the creation material appears in Genesis 1:26–27 with the statement that *humanity is created in the image of God.* Here scripture affirms the unique and precious quality of every person, male and female, as a bearer of the image of God. This is a clear and unambiguous affirmation of the coequal status of men and women as creatures of God. It is also a witness to the divine character as encompassing both maleness and femaleness, if indeed both men and women bear the image of God.

Creation in the image of God is not just a gift, it is also a responsibility. To be created in the image of God brings with it the commission to care for the earth, which follows in Genesis 1:28–30 (cf. 2:15). It was the practice of ancient kings to erect images of themselves to represent their sovereignty in the far-flung corners of their empires. The biblical writer has transferred this metaphor to the divine realm. In Genesis 1, God, who is truly sovereign over all creation, has chosen to place the divine image into human beings as the representatives not of some inherent human right of our own to exploit the creation for our own needs but as the representatives or trustees of God. So the commission to have dominion over the earth (v. 28) is a trusteeship of divine right, a trusteeship of God's own care for the creation and an entrusting to our stewardship of that care. Except for Genesis 1, this theme of human dominion is found explicitly only in Psalm 8. In both instances, exercise of dominion is accountable to God; it is not license for human indulgence. Thus, to have the gift of God's image is to have also the responsibility to show that image forth in relation to the whole of creation.

Another important theme in this material is *the affirmation of the goodness of creation.* At the end of the sixth day, "God saw everything that he had made, and behold, it was very good" (1:31). In biblical times this was a remarkable statement. Ancient cultures spoke of divine powers inhabiting all the realms of nature; hence, one often stood in fear and apprehension of the world and needed magic or incantations to protect oneself and appease the gods. In contrast, the Hebrews express the assurance that God's sovereign power has been used to create a world that is benevolent and trustworthy. Further, it is clear that God's intention is that the goodness of creation be experienced by all its parts, all persons and all nature. It was not to be good for some and bad for others and that's the breaks. Those who know the vision of God's good creation, therefore, cannot settle for a world where the desire of some for an excess of creation's good gifts begins to deny enough for others. To ensure that all participate in creation's goodness is a fundamental concern of Christian discipleship.

A third important theme is *the interrelatedness of creation.* Human beings are not self-sufficient. We are created for relationship to God, to others, and to nature. Genesis 2:18 tells us that God saw it was not good for the human creature to be alone. The story then goes on to express relationship with nature (garden, animals), as well as with other humans. Human relationship includes the possibility of sexual relationship as a part of God's creation. The first creature (called *'adam,* the general Hebrew word for humanity) is divided to make maleness and femaleness possible. There is no new creative forming-from-the-dust to make woman. Neither man nor woman exists until this point of sexual differentiation in the *'adam.* The Hebrew word often translated as helper *('ezer)* in 2:18 does not imply subordination. After all, the Bible often refers to God as our *'ezer.* It is better translated here as companion.

The Hebrew concept of creation is relational. Not only are we created as trustees of God to experience the goodness of creation, we are created to be in community with all creation. Only in this way can we experience God's intended wholeness *(shalom).* Each part of God's creation finds its fulfillment in interrelatedness with all. If some are denied wholeness, we all are diminished.

Opposed to this concept of creation as relational is a common and dangerous distortion of the biblical understanding of creation. It is *the distortion of hierarchical thinking about creation.* Over the centuries, in the church, the misuse of God's commission giving humanity dominion over the earth led to a hierarchical understanding that divided the relationship of the human to God and to nature. Hierarchical understanding operates something like this. Picture a ladder of categories. At the top is God, whose nature is pure spirit. At the bottom is the earth, whose nature is material. Already you have a polarity between the spiritual and the material, the divine and the bodily. Ranged in between are the other "orders" of creation: humans, animals, plants. The closer you get up the ladder to God, the higher is the moral worth attributed to that order of creation. Thus, the earth itself is far from God and of little worth. This is hardly in keeping with the pronouncement of God that the creation was all very good.

Early in the history of the Christian church a subdivided hierarchy became the standard: God, males, females, other races than white, Jews, animals, plants, and the earth itself. This hierarchical understanding of creation became the foundation for entire superstructures of racism, sexism, and anti-Semitism. It was the custom in the medieval law codes to list the killing of a Jew in the same section and with the same penalty as poaching the king's deer. Jews were thought guilty of deicide and therefore worth little more than animals. We all know that women and members of the nonwhite races have been slandered in the history of the church by defining their nature as closer to the bodily and animal orders of creation and therefore farther from God's spirit. They were said to occupy lower orders of creation, and this understanding in turn was used to justify slavery and the denial of ordination to women as well as a host of other racist and sexist actions. It has been suggested that in our century the poor have been added to the hierarchical list among those who are farther from God, while those who have been blessed with prosperity elevate themselves on the ladder to a position of greater closeness to God. The mere fact of being poor is treated by some as evidence of lower moral worth in the eyes of God.

If we had really understood the wholeness of the relational creation pictured in scripture, we could not have created that insidious hierarchical ladder. We would have understood that the welfare and the fullness of life for every part of creation is dependent on interrelationship and full participation of every other part. Creation is relational, not hierarchical.

The Brokenness of Creation

The Hebrew writers knew that the wholeness of creation which God intended was not a reality in human history. Thus, alongside the pictures of creation stands a story of the broken creation (Genesis 3). This story is closely attached to and flows from the garden creation story in Genesis 2. It is our first encounter with the biblical understanding of the nature and reality of sin.

Along with the other gifts of creation already discussed came the gift of human freedom. The man and the woman are given the capacity to make choices for themselves, and the choices are for either obedience or disobedience. It is the motif of the tree of knowledge in the midst of the garden (the tree of life does not figure in the story of chapter 3 until the end) which gives the possibility of human freedom. To eat of it is forbidden by God (Gen. 2:16–17). To have such freedom is a great gift, but with it comes human responsibility to live with the consequences of our choices. The consequence of eating from the tree of knowledge is said to be death.

What unfolds in the story of Genesis 3 is a drama that speaks to all of human existence concerning the meaning of our choices, the nature of sin, and the consequences of broken creation. It is important at the outset to note that this chapter does not exhaust the biblical perspective of sin. Sin is the word we use to describe how *shalom*, wholeness, gets broken. This story speaks of that brokenness in one important way, but we will see other aspects of sin later in Israel's story (e.g., covenant-breaking).

Since this is a story of human freedom and responsibility, it is important to note that the biblical text is quite clear that the serpent is simply one of the "wild creature[s] that the Lord God had made" (3:1). There is no coercive outside power of evil to take the man and the woman off the hook of responsibility for their own disobedience. We might think of the serpent as the tempting occasion for disobedience that comes into every human life.

In this case the temptation is to "be like God, knowing good and evil" (3:5). The aspect of sin highlighted in this story is the sin of overreach, attempting to go beyond the limits of our humanness to try for the prerogatives of God. Some theologians refer to this as the sin of pride. Pride is involved, but sin here is more than the attitude we associate with the word *pride*. It is the attempt to take destiny into one's own control as if we had no limits we must acknowledge

Knowledge of good and evil does not refer to the ability to make moral choices. After all, in being given the capacity to choose obedience or disobedience, humanity already has that capacity by virtue of God's creation. In Hebrew literature, pairs of opposites are used to bracket a whole category. East and west means everywhere; day and night means all the time; good and evil probably means everything. The temptation is to want to know everything that God knows. In Hebrew the verb *to know* does not mean just cognitive knowledge. To know something is to be related to the reality of what is known. It can almost mean "to experience" something. Thus, the man and the woman want to experience all that God does.

We must be careful in our interpretation here. This account does not imply that faithful life is against knowledge. It instead asks whether there are boundaries to human knowing that must be honored. How do we live in God's creation in a way that acknowledges the limits of our humanness and refuses to play God by reaching beyond those boundaries in ways that threaten to bring death? There may be forms of knowing that we attempt for our own human pride and self-centeredness which exact death-bringing penalties. One wonders if nuclear technology and some forms of genetic research are not flirting with these boundaries in ways that affect the entire human race. But apart from these dramatic issues, the biblical story speaks of the thousands of temptations to make choices that try to rearrange creation for our own benefit, only to bring death; biological, social, or spiritual.

The consequences of sin in this story are many. Death in the Old Testament is not simply biological. For *shalom* to be broken, for humans to be denied wholeness, is to experience death already. In this story the disobedient act immediately creates brokenness in the harmony of creation, as indicated by the appearance of shame and fear and guilt. In the creation story the man and woman were naked and not ashamed (2:25). Now they are ashamed of their nakedness and attempt to cover themselves (3:7). *Shame* is here the sign of brokenness in the openness of relationship between the man and the woman. When God finds the couple hiding from the divine presence, the man says he was afraid (3:10). *Fear* is here the sign of brokenness in the trustful relationship with God. Finally, there is a great buck-passing ceremony where the man and the woman try to pass responsibility on to others rather than face their own choice and its consequences (3:12–13). This is *guilt,* and it is here the sign of brokenness within one's own self.

In the penalties pronounced and the exile from the garden, the biblical writers are communicating to us their knowledge that we live in a broken world, far from the harmony of the garden. Many aspects of the reality of our lives remind us of what brokenness we have settled for when we were created for wholeness. One element of these verses on the consequences of sinful choice needs special comment. A part of the brokenness that the woman experiences is said to be her subservience to her husband ("he shall rule over you," 3:16). We must note carefully that scripture understands such subordination of women to be a sign of sin and not the intention of God in creation. Those of us whose story now includes the event of Jesus Christ, the new creation, must ask more seriously than in the past whether the church is in the business of enforcing the curses of sin in the old creation or of demonstrating the wholeness of relationship between men and women which God intended by acting as the community of new creation.

TOWARD THE PROMISE

We have spent a good deal of time on the opening chapters of the Old Testament. From these chapters we know much of the nature of God as Creator and ourselves as creatures, but as the story moves forward, Creator and creatures are alienated from one another. In the chapters that follow, the alienation seems to grow. Sin abounds and its consequences grow more violent. In the Cain and Abel story, violence is directed toward an innocent brother (Genesis 4). In the story of the flood, sin and violence have reached universal proportions and God is sorry that the world was created (Gen. 6:5–7). At the tower of Babel, humanity attempts to assault the heavens themselves for their own glory ("let us make a name for ourselves," Gen. 11:4). The gulf between God and humanity seems to grow greater, as does the brokenness in humanity itself. In each story there are consequences of sin: Cain's exile, the flood, the scattering and confusion of language. But in each story there is a sign that in spite of sin God continues to care and to act with grace: God marks Cain for protection, saves Noah, guarantees the natural order with the rainbow.

After the tower of Babel story, there is no immediate sign of God's care. We are dramatically suspended for a moment. Where can this escalation of sin and alienation end? It is then that we are shifted from stories that speak of all humanity to the story of a single man and woman and the people who spring from them. Genesis 12 begins the story of Abraham and Sarah. Significantly, their story begins with a promise, and it becomes clear that the story of this people of promise is the sign of God's grace. God acts to bridge the gap through relationship to a particular people. The story of God's relationship to this people is now the subject of the rest of the Old Testament. By beginning with creation and broken creation, the scripture reminds us that this people is not to be an end in itself but a means of God's grace to "all the families of the earth" (Gen. 12:3).

2

FROM PROMISE
TO DELIVERANCE

* * *

For Israel's historians and poets, Israel as a people came to birth in the experience of God's deliverance from bondage in Egypt. These exodus events, beginning with the call of Moses (Exodus 3) and culminating with the deliverance at the sea (Exodus 14–15), were for Israel the central salvation events of their faith. God was there revealed to them in new and decisive ways. The common experience of God's saving grace began the formation of a people of faith. Moses' leadership modeled certain roles of faithful service to God and people. Exodus showed a pattern of God's grace that is experienced in other settings and times and is remembered in Israel's worship.

Yet, if Exodus is at the center of Israel's faith identity, it is not entirely without preparation. The stories of God's promise to Abraham and the lives of Israel's ancestors lived in relation to that promise are found in Genesis 12–50 and form an important prologue to the beginning of the salvation history in Exodus. In these stories, peoplehood is promised but not yet realized. In fact, it is only as Israel's storytellers looked back long after coming from bondage in Egypt to final settlement in the promised land that those stories of the promise were fully understood and could be told as a part of Israel's story.

The Call to Sojourn

After chronicling the growth of sin and alienation in
all humankind (Genesis 3–11), the biblical story abruptly
shifts to the call of a single man and his wife from whom
a whole people will come. It is clear that the biblical
writers understood this story of Abraham and Sarah as
the beginning of the story of Israel, whom God called
into existence to be an instrument of grace in this sinful
and broken world. It is a story that begins with a calling
and a promise.

In Genesis 12:1 God calls Abram (his name is later
expanded to Abraham) to leave "your country and your
kindred and your father's house." It is a summons to
radical separation from those things that usually made
for security in biblical times: land, family, and inheritance (the word *house* here means household in the sense
of all of a family's retainers and goods).

In place of that material security is given God's promise. "Go . . . to the land that I will show you. And I will
make of you a great nation . . . and by you all the families
of the earth shall bless themselves" (Gen. 12:1–3). The
promise to Abraham and those who came after him has
three elements: land, descendants, and mission.
Abraham is given no script for how these things will
come to pass. He must place his trust in God's grace and
go forward in answer to God's call.

It would be a mistake to see the promise only in terms
of Abraham; the promise also tells us something of God.
The three elements indicate to Abraham and to us a God
who is not limited by place (calls from one land to another) or by time (spans generations) and who is acting
on the most universal scale (the blessing of all human-

kind). It is Abraham who becomes a part of God's history, not God who becomes a part of Abraham's.

Those who receive God's promise are summoned to a particular life-style. The word used most often in Genesis to describe this is *sojourning.* This is a term in biblical Hebrew used to describe persons who live in a place, perhaps for an extended period of time, but are not totally defined by that place. They are aliens, outsiders, always looking toward a permanent home that has not yet been given. Sojourning is sometimes translated as pilgrimage (Gen. 47:9, KJV), and this communicates the sense of purpose that is a part of sojourning, a purpose which comes from God. To be a sojourner in the biblical sense is to trust in God's promise that there is a place for us even when this is not immediately apparent. It is to trust in God's promise that the divine purpose is at work even if it must be our descendants who see its fruits. It is to know that we are a part of God's plan for the redemption of all creation and not merely our own.

Following the promise given to Abraham, the stories of Israel's ancestors in the remaining chapters of Genesis form an epic of the adventures of the promise. Story after story raises doubts about the reliability of the promise. Abraham gets poorer land, while Lot gets the rich land around Sodom and Gomorrah. Sarah grows old and is still barren. After Isaac is miraculously born in Abraham and Sarah's old age, God tells Abraham to take the child out and sacrifice him. Abraham is described as righteous, but God's promise gets handed on to Jacob, a conniving swindler who is driven from the land for his misdeeds by his brother Esau. These are only a few of the stories, but they are almost all designed to show how God's promise is sure even when human events raise doubts. God's promise can also move forward through many different human agents, righteous or conniving. It is God's faithfulness to the promise that counts.

Finally the story brings us to Joseph and his brothers (Genesis 37; 39–50). On the surface it is the story of a young man who constantly triumphs over adversity and finally comes into a position of great power in Egypt. Hebrew tradition is justly proud of one of its own who makes good and who, in addition, forgives his brothers. The tradition sees God still moving in these events. Joseph says to his brothers in 50:20, "You meant evil against me; but God meant it for good, to bring it about that many people should be kept alive."

There is, however, a difference in the story of Joseph. God is more hidden. Nowhere does God speak to Joseph as to Abraham and Jacob. Nowhere is the promise revealed and reaffirmed to Joseph or any of his brothers. God's activity is entirely through human agency, and modern readers are often more comfortable with this greater human role. But as God grows more hidden and human action more prominent, a danger arises, even in the midst of good intentions.

Joseph brings to Egypt his father, Jacob, and his eleven brothers with their families. In Genesis 47 they all arrive to "sojourn," but Pharaoh invites them to "settle" and they do. The landless possess land for the first time, and one of their own, Joseph, possesses political power as well. Famine is upon the land and Joseph's intention is to preserve life, but in providing food he first takes people's money (47:14–15), then their cattle (vs. 16–17), and finally their fields, with the people made slaves upon their own land (vs. 18–25). Only the land of the priests does not become centralized under Pharaoh's control.

All this prepares the way for the day when "there

arose a new king over Egypt, who did not know Joseph"
(Ex. 1:8), and Israel's ancestors, the descendants of Joseph
and his family, also become slaves. God and God's promises have grown dim in the story and are now eclipsed.
Israel has been in Egypt for four centuries, with no stories of God or the children of Israel. It is a time of bondage and suffering, ironically made possible by centralized
royal power put in place by Joseph. It is a terrible reminder of the dangers of "settlement" and "power"
when God's promise grows dim. Human action is not
tempered by a sense of God's constant gift, and with the
best of intentions the tools of tyranny are put in place.

The God Who Saves

Over a period of several generations the ancestors of
Israel have been reduced to a position of slavery under
cruel Egyptian pharaohs (Ex. 1:1–14). But the Hebrews
in bondage maintain some spirit and resourcefulness.
The story of the Hebrew midwives outwitting Pharaoh
in Exodus 1:15–22 is a bittersweet tale of women's courage and resourcefulness contrasted with the brutal and
dehumanizing power of a tyrant. We are to make no
mistake: Pharaoh represents the epitome of oppressive
power in the world.

The central question of the story quickly becomes
"Where does real power lie?" The Hebrews are powerless to deliver themselves from their own oppressed condition. It is God who takes the initiative. God hears their
cries, calls Moses to be the instrument of deliverance,
demonstrates power even over Pharaoh and mighty
Egypt, and leads the people forth in a great pillar of
cloud and fire.

The great dramatic climax comes when the Hebrews

are seemingly cut off at the sea with the Egyptians in pursuit. In this apparently hopeless situation they are miraculously delivered through the sea and the Egyptians are destroyed. What has happened? To the Hebrews the answer was theological. God delivered them "with a mighty hand and an outstretched arm" (Deut. 26:8). They who were "no people" became "God's people." Those whose way seemed totally cut off now found the future open before them.

In this central experience something is revealed to Israel—and to us—about the character of God. This is first seen clearly in the dramatic encounter of Moses with God in the burning bush (Exodus 3). God says, "I have seen the affliction of my people who are in Egypt, and have heard their cry because of their taskmasters; I know their sufferings, and I have come down to deliver them out of the hand of the Egyptians" (Ex. 3:7–8). It is significant in this passage that God is revealed as one who sees and hears. This points to a caring God who takes note of Israel's oppression and suffering. Remarkably, in this verse God also claims to experience it with them. As we saw in the last chapter, the Hebrew verb *to know* means far more than the intellectual knowledge our word implies. For the Hebrews, to know meant a total involvement with and experiencing of that which is known. For God to *know* Israel's suffering is a revelation of unique involvement of the divine with the human condition. This is the beginning point of the Christian conception of a suffering God. God suffers as we suffer. God participates in our pain and brokenness. Of course, this concept receives its fullest expression in the crucifixion.

From here on, Israelite faith recognizes its God as one who especially loves and cares for the oppressed, the afflicted, the poor, and the hungry. Text after text echoes the sentiment of Psalm 12:5, " 'Because the poor are despoiled, because the needy groan, I will now arise,' says the Lord; 'I will place him in the safety for which he longs.' " The God of Old Testament faith is especially the God of the dispossessed. God will not forget or forsake them. It is within this tradition that Jesus stands in his radical ministry to the outcasts and the dispossessed of New Testament times. "As you did it to one of the least of these my brethren, you did it to me" (Matt. 25:40).

God's love for the powerless does not, however, imply an acceptance of their condition. As Exodus 3:8 makes clear, God loves them in order to deliver them. The exodus events form the central witness for Israel to a God who saves.

At several points in the Old Testament the tradition has preserved statements of faith that recite the great salvation events of Israel's story (Deut. 26:5–11; Josh. 24). These are the events of Israel's salvation history, the mighty acts of God, and exodus is always first among them. In God's saving activity, Israel comes to know God not only as one who stands behind the ongoing created order of things (the God who creates and blesses) but as one who has entered history in a decisive way to effect salvation. Alongside the universal reality of the Creator God stands the particularity of the God who entered history and became a part of our story. God chooses to relate to a group of insignificant slaves and call them into being as God's own people.

It is impossible to make such a God remote and removed from the realities of human events, especially those manifesting the brokenness of the human condition. The God who saves is to be found precisely where brokenness is most evident and where, therefore, the need of God's grace is the greatest. This is not where

most churches tend to seek the presence and activity of
God.

EXODUS AS LIBERATION

God's saving activity in the exodus events resulted in
liberation of the Hebrews from enslavement to an oppressive power. This also established a relationship between Israel and God the Liberator. To speak of exodus
as liberation serves to guard against too easy a spirituali-
zation of the salvation events. God's deliverance is a political event as well as a spiritual one.

This basic image of God's deliverance, seen in exodus
images, is finding powerful new expression in the current liberation theologies. These theologies are rooted in
the struggles of American blacks, Native Americans,
Latin Americans, Africans, and Asians against systems
of poverty and oppression that strip persons of their own
humanity and leave them without hope. The exodus
drama of God's intervention against hostile forces to
effect deliverance provides the basis for hope and action
in the contexts out of which those theologies come.

Several important areas of insight become clear when
we view the exodus events with a liberation perspective.

1. Exodus as liberation reminds us of God's opposition
to the powers of the world when they are exercised for
oppression. In the world of the Hebrew historians and
storytellers, the pharaoh of mighty Egypt was the epitome of earthly power. As is often the case with such
powers, claims to greatness were supported by religious
justifications. The pharaoh was himself said to be a god.
Part of the drama of the exodus story is the confrontation
of Israel's God with this Egyptian god-king. Is our God

the equal of such obvious power? Can a God who identifies with oppressed slaves be more powerful than the
forces that serve the king of such a mighty empire?

It is important to be clear that Pharaoh and his representatives are recognized in the story as tyrants who
dehumanize and exploit others for their own selfish purposes. The tyrant in this story is capable of genocide (Ex.
1:8–22). As is often the case with oppressors, Pharaoh and
his loyal subjects live in fear of those they victimize
(1:12).

This recognition of Pharaoh as an oppressor in his
own right is important because of the confusion which
often arises later in the story when it is said that God
"hardens Pharaoh's heart." Actually the story says sometimes that God hardened his heart (7:3) and sometimes
that Pharaoh hardened his own heart (8:15). We should
not imagine that the story intends to imply that Pharaoh
is not responsible for his own oppressive actions. Pharaoh was an inhuman tyrant before the struggle with God
through Moses began over the liberation of the Hebrew
slaves. To have God harden Pharaoh's heart is simply the
storyteller's way of heightening the message that even
with the greatness of Egypt's power it is God who is
truly sovereign over history. It does not make God responsible for the consequences of Pharaoh's own choice
for oppressive action.

In the conflict with Pharaoh, the message is firmly
planted in Israel's faith that those who trust in the Lord
are never hopeless and helpless no matter what their
worldly circumstances might be. The activity of God is
present in the world in those forces that challenge tyrants and refuse to accept the exercise of oppressive
power as legitimate.

2. Exodus as liberation means moving out. This is the literal meaning of exodus. For the Hebrews, deliverance from bondage meant being uprooted, leaving the only home known to that generation and journeying into unfamiliar lands. They could not build structures but lived in tents which could be packed and set up in another place if the pillar of cloud or fire should move out before them.

In such circumstances, bondage looked like security to some. They wished they had stayed in Egypt or hoped to stay at one of the oases where comfortable camp was made. They "murmured" against Moses for moving them in the first place. Nevertheless, exodus journeying with God meant readiness to move forward.

When the people of God, from biblical times to our own, recognize their beginnings in this exodus journeying, their own life will be marked by a creative restlessness. It involves a willingness to see where God is moving ahead of us and to move forward. In our survey of the Old Testament, we will see many who stood ready to follow God's lead and left for us a witness and a challenge to be the exodus community in our own churches.

Unfortunately, the churches of America display a tendency to camp around the status quo. We become comfortable with the patterns of our church life. We do not wish to hear the summons that uproots our existence. We do not wish to see the pillar that moves out, leaving our carefully built structures behind. This attitude has made the church in our time an ally (witting or unwitting) of the cultural status quo. Few would say of us, "These . . . who have turned the world upside down have come here also" (Acts 17:6).

3. Briefly we can note that, in Exodus, liberation was not into the promised land but into the wilderness. The Hebrews escaped bondage only to encounter the harsh realities of the desert. Inadequate food and water, hostile enemies, and doubts about their goal made for crises. They were liberated, but the wilderness into which they were delivered was a place full of hardships and struggles.

The life of faith for Israel and for us is not a safe-conduct around struggle and difficulty. The wilderness became a time for learning what it means to rely on God's providence. Salvation still leaves the people of God in the harsh realities of the world, but the difference is God's presence with them. Those who seek salvation to remove them from the world's struggles are like those who preferred the security of bondage to the difficult journey of those liberated to become God's faithful people.

4. Remembrance of exodus in Israel was not only a matter of hope, it was a matter of humility. Over and over again in the Old Testament texts, Israel is admonished in a manner similar to this: "You shall remember that you were a slave in the land of Egypt, and the Lord your God redeemed you" (Deut. 15:15). The faithful community is reminded that nothing it has is of its own doing. All is the gift of God. Even its deliverance was not because of unique status before God, but simply because God loved Israel (Deut. 7:7–8).

The community of faith from biblical times onward has always found it tempting, when it experiences prosperity, to attribute success pridefully to its own efforts and worth. Blessing is regarded as an achievement. Exodus was a reminder to Israel in the times of blessing that its own roots were among the dispossessed. Remembrance of exodus was a corrective to pride and self-sufficiency.

Exodus as a Pattern of Faith

For Israel, exodus did not remain simply as an event tied to its moorings in a distant historical memory. The experience of deliverance from bondage in Egypt became a model for understanding the experience of God's salvation in subsequent generations. Exodus was seen as a paradigm, or pattern, for the facing of any crisis in the context of Israel's faith. The Hebrews had been faced with a seemingly hopeless situation. They were brought up to the edge of the sea, with Pharaoh's army closing in behind, and where there seemed to be no way into the future, God opened up a way. Distress became unexpected deliverance, not through Israel's efforts but through God's. Israel applied this pattern beyond that one historic moment at the sea. This pattern of distress becoming deliverance was applied in all experiences of crisis and served to undergird the confidence that God is always present.

The pattern has three elements. Interestingly, one of the places in the Old Testament where these can be seen most clearly in use is in the book of Psalms. Since the psalms are drawn from Israel's worship life, they reflect the heart of Israelite faith and show all three elements of the pattern clearly.

1. All persons and communities experience *situations of distress.* Human experience naturally includes crises when the future is not clear and there seem no possibilities for hope or life. In those moments persons feel pow-

erless to find a way into the future. Many psalms express this element of the pattern, the laments. They speak candidly of grief, rage, doubt, and despair. With the exception of Psalm 88, however, all these laments move toward and express trust and confidence in God's deliverance. They reflect knowledge of the exodus pattern of faith.

2. *God's unexpected deliverance* is the second element of the pattern. Exodus faith knows of God's power and grace, which brings life and possibility for the future where only death and despair seemed to reign. The psalms of thanksgiving are celebrations of the experience of deliverance looking back on crisis and distress. Just as Israel at worship holds up the reality of distress, it also proclaims the word of deliverance. It is worth noting that Israel is well aware that the path into God's future may open up in unexpected ways. The shape of the new possibility that comes from God is often different from the deliverance for which we wish. The trust is that with God new life will be possible even from the moment of worst crisis.

3. The third element of the exodus pattern of faith is *Israel's response in community.* A community that has known and acknowledged the experience of God's salvation cannot live like other communities. What can it mean to be a delivered people? Israel's response was both in worship and in ethics. In worship Israel remembered and celebrated God's great acts of salvation, including exodus. In its way of living and relating (ethics), Israel lived out the implications of being God's people. Here we have gone beyond the scope of this chapter, because to understand Israel's response to the exodus experience of deliverance fully we must go on to Sinai and an understanding of covenant. That will be the subject of the next

chapter. To comment briefly on our pattern, we can note that here too the psalms reflect it. Festival psalms that remember and celebrate Israel's faith history can be found, along with prophetic psalms that challenge Israel's moral life.

We can conclude our discussion of exodus as a pattern of faith in Israel by noting that this same pattern is still prominent in understandings of our Christian faith centered in the death and resurrection of Jesus Christ. Consider the following diagram of the exodus pattern and its parallels.

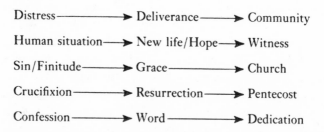

Distress ⟶ Deliverance ⟶ Community

Human situation ⟶ New life/Hope ⟶ Witness

Sin/Finitude ⟶ Grace ⟶ Church

Crucifixion ⟶ Resurrection ⟶ Pentecost

Confession ⟶ Word ⟶ Dedication

The pattern that emerged from the exodus experience leading to the formation of community at Sinai is still at the heart of Christian theology. In classical terms we speak of sin or finitude as the source of our distress, grace as the experience of deliverance and new life, and the church as the community of response. The same pattern is reflected in the death and resurrection of Jesus followed by the calling forth of a community of response. In many patterns of church liturgy this exodus pattern may be seen in the movement from confession of our distress, hearing of the word of new possibility in scripture and preaching, and responding in prayer, gifts, and sending forth. The exodus experience and its reverberations throughout the history of our Judeo-Christian faith are still present at the core of our faith today.

SALVATION AS PHYSICAL AND SPIRITUAL

As a final insight to be highlighted from the exodus experience, we must call attention to the comprehensive understanding of salvation demonstrated in this story. Here, at the very birth of Israel as a people, it is made clear that God's salvation involves a concern for physical as well as spiritual well-being. Exodus is not just a spiritual metaphor. Indeed, it is out of Israel's experience of God's concrete physical deliverance that a new relationship to God is possible.

In considering the exodus tradition, the argument is sometimes made that everyone experiences bondage of some sort and is in need of liberation. While this is true, it runs the risk of trivializing or spiritualizing bondage and oppression. Some persons focus upon psychological or spiritual alienation in such a way as to excuse our lack of serious effort on behalf of those experiencing physical suffering in the world. We must be aware of the inward-turning, individualized character of this response as compared to the biblical concept. The biblical under-standing of bondage includes physical and spiritual ele-ments. Likewise, the biblical concept of salvation is phys-ical and spiritual. God desires our wholeness in every respect, and the exodus story tells us of God's action to make it possible.

Exodus reminds us that we must not fall victim to the easy temptation of seeking to save the world's soul while its body is in pain. God's salvation is the promise of deliverance for spirit and body, and God is active to bring us fullness of life as whole persons. We must be reminded that spiritual alienation in our time is wedded to great systems of physical dehumanization that crush the spirit of those who suffer, corrupt the spirit of those who oppress, and dull the spirit of those who refuse to see and hear.

3

You Shall
Be My People

* * *

In the dramatic events at the sea (Exodus 14–15) the Hebrews experienced deliverance, but deliverance was into the wilderness and not the promised land. They escaped bondage only to encounter the harsh realities of wilderness struggle. At times there was not enough food or water (Exodus 16–17). The journey was strenuous and long. In the midst of these hardships, the people "murmured" against Moses and longed to be back in the slavery of Egypt, where they had food (Ex. 16:2–3). To the Hebrews, as to many since their time, the security of bondage looked preferable to the struggles of freedom; many will choose the path of minimal security if the way to freedom looks difficult and challenging. In all these wilderness crises, God working through Moses provided the resources the people needed and rebuked them for their lack of faith. They were delivered but were not yet a people. That was yet to be accomplished when the Hebrews finally made camp at Mount Sinai (Exodus 19).

The deliverance from Egypt represented God's initiative toward Israel, but at Sinai the motley group of former slaves was given the opportunity to respond by becoming a community covenanted with God. They had experienced God's grace. How were they to live in acknowledgment of that grace? Sinai's central concern was the shaping of a community of faith that chose to harness its future to divine power in covenant obedience. Israel accepted that demanding relationship and began in that encampment to discover its full meaning. At Sinai, Israel became God's people, called upon to embody the experience of God's deliverance in a community for whom love of God was intimately bound with love of neighbor (Lev. 19:18). Israel was liberated *from* oppression and suffering but was liberated *for* community and mutual responsibility.

An Alternative Community of Covenant

The life of Israel as a faith community was definitively shaped by a distinct consciousness of religious and social reality that set it apart from the prevailing cultures of the surrounding ancient world. Israel understood itself called to life as an alternative community, clearly different from the models of community seen in the neighboring cultures—Egyptian, Mesopotamian, Canaanite—of the biblical period. There were, of course, influences from these cultures, but at the level of basic perspective Israel was not to be "like the nations." When Israel was tempted to emulate the nations in ways that compromised the covenant understanding, God's covenant messengers, the prophets, called them back to faithfulness.

The beginning point for this understanding of alternative community was the establishment of covenant at Mount Sinai in the time of Moses. Covenant is the Old Testament term to designate this understanding of alternative community. The Hebrew word for covenant, *berith*, was a common word used for an agreement or a contract. It is used elsewhere in the Bible in this common meaning, sometimes for agreements between human partners (Jacob and Laban), but even for the promises given by God to the ancestors (Genesis 15). From Mount Sinai onward, covenant becomes the designation for that special relationship established between Yahweh and Israel as a response to God's salvation in the exodus events. The Ten Commandments in Exodus 20:2 begin the most important of covenant texts with this acknowledgment, "I am the Lord your God, who brought you out of the land of Egypt, out of the house of bondage."

For Israel the alternative understanding of covenant emerged and was defined over against the imperial reality of Egypt from which Israel was delivered. Egypt was formed in the pattern of the great cultures of that time. The power of the nation was intimately tied to the power of the gods. When Egypt is weak the gods are said to be weak, but when Egypt is strong the gods are said to be strong. The power of the gods of Egypt is measured in the world by the strength of Egypt's military might, Egypt's economic strength, and Egypt's cultural greatness. Over against this imperial reality, Israel emerges with an alternative pattern of community that is quite distinct in its religion, politics, and economics. With only slight variations, this covenant model served as well to set Israel apart from the later empires, kingdoms, and cultures it encountered.

In what follows we will examine the way in which the covenant model understands religion, politics, and economics and see the relationship of these in faithful community. It is our belief that this covenant model is very similar to the alternative community demonstrated in the life of the earliest church following Pentecost. For that reason we will refer at brief points to New Testament reflections of the covenant model for faith community.

THE COVENANT GOD

The origin of the covenantal understanding is religious. It arises out of a growing experience of relationship to a God characterized by freedom, vulnerability, and fidelity.

Israel's God is defined first and foremost by divine freedom and not by the fate of any particular culture or nation. This conception of the radical *freedom of God* emerges in opposition to the nationally defined gods of imperial triumphalism in Egypt. The God of covenant is so free that God can choose to enter relationship with a people who are merely a band of slaves with no standing, no power, no influence in the world. This God is defined by freely offered compassion to those who, by the world's definition, are the helpless, the oppressed, and the dispossessed.

It is the covenant God who says in Exodus 33:19, "I will show mercy on whom I will show mercy." We resist this statement because we usually take it to indicate divine arbitrariness rather than divine freedom. The biblical tradition stresses the fact that we have become God's people not out of special merit but only out of freely given grace. "It was not because you were more in number than any other people that the Lord set his love upon you and chose you . . . but it is because the Lord loves you" (Deut. 7:7). We do not lay claim upon God. Even our greatest righteousness does not obligate God, so God is not possessed by any people, tradition, or culture. Knowledge of the freedom of God is the corrective to our natural tendency to limit God by suggesting that God is obligated to reward the faithful with blessings (e.g., economic prosperity or political dominance).

Those concerned for the social implications of faith have undervalued the biblical notion of God's freedom. Walter Brueggemann, in his book *The Prophetic Imagination* (pp. 16–17), reminds us that in the liberation of Israel from Egypt the overturning of an oppressive social system is linked to new understanding of the God who does this thing.

> In place of the gods of Egypt, creatures of the imperial consciousness, Moses discloses Yahweh, the sovereign one who acts in his lordly freedom, is extrapolated from no social reality, and is captive to no social perception but acts from his own person toward his own purposes. At the same time, Moses dismantles the politics of oppression and exploitation by countering it with a politics of justice and compassion. . . . The participants in the Exodus found themselves . . . involved in the intentional formation of a new social community to match the vision of God's freedom.

The freedom of God is asserted over and over again in the biblical tradition. It is the radically free God who reminds Job out of the whirlwind that even his perfect righteousness and his suffering do not coerce God (Job 38). It is this same God who forgave the Ninevites, much to the disgust of Jonah (Jonah 4). This is the God known to the prophet of the exile, who saw in the Persian king Cyrus the instrument of God's salvation and called him God's anointed (Isa. 45:1–7). Imagine a God free to choose and work through a nonbeliever and the king of a pagan empire! This has some implications for the surprising places we might find God at work in our own time. Finally, we should mention that it is of the freedom of God that Paul writes when speaking of justification by faith alone in Romans 9:14–16: "What shall we say then?

Is there injustice on God's part? By no means! For he says to Moses, 'I will have mercy on whom I have mercy. . . .' So it depends not upon [human] will or exertion, but upon God's mercy."

God is not only free but has chosen to use that freedom to enter into relationship. Freedom alone could result in the picture of an aloof, uncaring God. This is not at all the picture in covenantal texts. Instead we see a God whose freedom has been used to become vulnerable to human experience. This *vulnerability of God* was the subject of discussion in chapter 2. We spoke of Exodus 3:7 and God's participation in our suffering as revealed in the exodus experience. Here we need only remind ourselves that this same care and compassion and involvement in our condition is a part of the character of the covenanting God.

A remarkable word often used to show this side of God's character is the Hebrew word usually translated as "compassion." It is a word derived from the Hebrew word for *womb*. God's compassion is a kind of "womb love." Here the biblical witness has chosen an image pointing to the total involvement and interrelationship of two lives, as when a mother carries a child. Thus, God's compassion is a metaphor of the womb to speak to us of God's total involvement with God's people. It is an image of life participating in life, coming together as one in covenant relationship. "Can a woman forget her sucking child, that she should have no compassion on the son of her womb? Even these may forget, yet I will not forget you" (Isa. 49:15).

Alongside freedom and vulnerability stands the *fidelity of God*. The covenant-making at Sinai represents the beginning of a story of God's faithfulness that stretches on through the whole Old Testament. Israel can choose to break covenant and therefore sever the relationship, but God's love and the offer of that relationship are never withdrawn. Nowhere is it suggested that covenant is anything less than a permanent and unconditional offer initiated freely by God.

The Hebrew word for this covenant faithfulness is *ḥesed*, "steadfast love." Psalm 136 expresses it best by using the refrain over and over: "For [God's] steadfast love endures for ever."

The fidelity of God to the freely given covenant relationship becomes the basis in Israel's faith for justice, righteousness, and wholeness *(shalom)*. These qualities can only exist in history if they are based in a radically free God who is not limited by history, yet is trustworthy in relationship to that history. Any attempt to locate justice and its related qualities in the social order itself is destined to fail, for even the most noble attempts at just community experience brokenness; Israel's own history is eloquent testimony to that. Even the covenant community fell into patterns of oppression and privilege. Hope was possible because God in whom justice rests was free and faithful. Thus, the prophets could announce both judgment and hope in the name of that covenant God. Wherever the attempt is made to limit or domesticate the freedom of God or to suggest that God is not faithful in the divine caring, you can be certain that privilege and oppression in the social order are not far behind.

THE POLITICS OF COVENANT

In the covenantal understanding of community, Israel adopted a *politics of justice* that contrasted sharply with the centralized and hierarchical power characteristic of the nations that surrounded Israel. The basis of Israel's covenant politics was the equal claim of all persons before God. The use of power and the making of decisions were to reflect this equal worth as fully as possible.

The covenant community was to resist the granting of special privilege in society to an elite group. Even the great Moses was judged and denied access to the promised land when he began to claim special privilege before God as a prerogative of leadership. The law codes show Israel's concern to structure life as a covenant community in a manner that ensured the fullest possible participation of all persons. The denial of full participation in the community to any person or group was considered a serious breach of the integrity of the entire community.

Recent studies of the sociology of early Israel have shown that Israel's social structure in the earliest periods was characterized by an egalitarian and decentralized system of authority. This system of covenant federation, tribes, clans, and families, represented a kind of dispersed, decentralized political structure that is in sharp contrast to the patterns of other ancient cultures. It tended to operate from the grass roots up rather than from the top down.

It is the principle of justice that is to guard the integrity of this political order. It is justice that is concerned for the full worth and participation of persons in the social order. Israel's justice is to reflect God's justice in its valuing of all persons. In attempting to embody this principle, Israel structured its life in a nonhierarchical fashion and resisted the notion of permanent offices for the exercise of power (e.g., kings or generals). This political system was buttressed by an elaborate judicial system to ensure the access of all, especially the weak, to justice within the community.

The earliest church as seen in the New Testament reflects a similar alternative pattern. Jesus rejected the authoritarian and hierarchical patterns of society in his time. "You know that the rulers of the Gentiles lord it over them, and their great men exercise authority over them. It shall not be so among you; but whoever would be great among you must be your servant" (Matt. 20:25–26). Following Jesus' acceptance of all persons regardless of social status, membership and leadership in the early church crossed the bounds of culturally accepted patterns of class, race, culture, and sex. All had access to God through Christ (Gal. 3:28) in what has been called a tradition of coequal discipleship. The patterns of the early church were, like Israel's covenant, intended to be participatory and not hierarchical or authoritarian.

THE ECONOMICS OF COVENANT

The third element of the covenantal pattern is an *economics of equality*. Here we are dealing with the use and distribution of resources within the social structure of the community of faith. The principle by which Israel tried to organize its economic life is captured in the story of the manna, which follows the experience of deliverance at the sea in Exodus 16. When God sends manna as food for the people's need in the wilderness, we are told that "the people of Israel . . . gathered, some more, some less. But when they measured it with an omer, he that gathered much had nothing over, and he that gathered little had no lack; each gathered according to what he could eat" (vs. 17–18). That conception of equal access to community resources according to need formed the cornerstone for an economics of equality which is spelled out in radical terms during Israel's early life as a covenant community.

For Israel, covenant was expressed not only in love of God but in love of neighbor, and in particular the neighbor in need. Over and over again, the earliest law codes emphasize the importance of systems of distribution of the resources of the community that allowed all to have access to those goods that would fulfill their basic human needs. This concern to supply the necessities of life for all extended even to the stranger and the sojourner.

Much can be learned from the seriousness with which Israel attempted to establish concrete structures of care for human needs. Because God had identified with the dispossessed, the care of those in need was not regarded in Israel as an act of individual, voluntary benevolence. The poor, the hungry, and the needy were entitled to the care of the community. Underlying this practice was the assumption that genuine need was due to a breakdown in the equitable distribution of community resources or to a social status over which individuals had no control (e.g., widows and orphans). Thus, the responsibility for initiative lay with the privileged rather than with the dispossessed themselves, even as God had taken the initiative to deliver Israel.

The rights of the poor and those in need are delineated most clearly in the law codes of the Old Testament. Here, concern is taken out of the realm of voluntary charity. The clearest statement appears in Deuteronomy 15:4–5, 7–8, 10–11:

> There will be no poor among you . . . if only you will obey the voice of the Lord your God. . . . If there is among you a poor man, one of your brethren, in any of your towns within your land which the Lord your God gives you, you shall not harden your heart or shut your hand against your

poor brother, but you shall open your hand to him, and lend him sufficient for his need. . . . You shall give to him freely, and your heart shall not be grudging. . . . For the poor will never cease out of the land; therefore, I command you, You shall open wide your hand to your brother, to the needy and to the poor.

This passage suggests that if the demands of the covenant were fully embodied, there would be no poverty and need, but since Israel like all human communities is less than perfect, some of its inhabitants will inevitably be poor. Therefore, God's people are commanded to care for them. This task is part of what it means to be the people of God; it is not an optional activity.

Adequate food was particularly regarded as an inherent right for every person. Major attention in Israel's covenantal law codes is given to provision of food for those in need. The poor could eat grapes in a neighbor's vineyard or pluck grain when passing by a field (Deut. 23:24–25). They also had the right to glean in fields and vineyards and to take any sheaves left behind. Owners were urged, for the sake of the poor and hungry, not to be too efficient in their harvest (Lev. 19:9–10; 23:22; Deut. 24:19; Ruth 2:1–3). Anything that grew up in fallow fields belonged to the poor (Ex. 23:10–11), and they were to receive the tithe of every third year (Deut. 14:28–29; 26:12).

The Old Testament law codes also provided for the protection of the poor and powerless in the socioeconomic system. Persons were urged to lend money to the poor (Deut. 15:7–8), but the law prohibited the taking of interest (Ex. 22:25). Garments, or other items necessary for survival, if taken from the poor as security for a debt, were to be returned each night so that a person might not have to face the night without a cloak (Ex. 22:26–27;

Deut. 24:10–13). So that the poor would not remain permanently in debt, the law called for the remission of debts after seven years (Deut. 15:1–2); if a poor man sold himself into servitude because of debts, he was to be given freedom in the seventh year (Lev. 25:39–55), and he should not then be sent out empty-handed but given provision from the flocks and the harvest (Deut. 15:12–15).

A special word must be said about the biblical concept of the jubilee year. Israel knew that the covenant would be broken and that societal structures for corporate care would be perverted and abused. Thus, the law included a provision for every seventh year to be a sabbath year; and after seven sabbath years, the fiftieth year was to be a year of jubilee. In these years the inequities of the social order were to be rectified so that justice might be restored in the covenant community.

In particular, the jubilee ideal called for a year of letting the land lie fallow, the remission of all debts, the liberation of slaves, and the return of family property to its original owner (Leviticus 25). Many have debated whether such provisions were ever fully carried out. No doubt the jubilee represented an ideal standard of radical societal renewal to restore wholeness and equity. But even if utopian, jubilee has come to represent the kind of daring vision called for on the part of God's people. There is considerable evidence that many faithful figures of the Old and New Testaments, such as Jeremiah and Jesus, took this ideal standard of jubilee seriously as the just society for which God calls us to work even if society at large refuses the vision.

Most important, jubilee became an essential ingredient in the biblical vision of God's future. The language of jubilee is used to describe that final "day of the Lord" when justice and righteousness shall be established in their fullness. It is the age when swords shall be beaten into plowshares (Isa. 2:4) and "the wolf shall dwell with the lamb" (Isa. 11:6). Jubilee represents that vision of peace and equity which must always motivate the people of God to renewed efforts in their own present. That some of our own national forebears shared that vision must surely be attested by their choosing an inscription for the Liberty Bell from the jubilee laws of Leviticus: "Proclaim liberty throughout all the land unto all the inhabitants thereof" (Lev. 25:10, KJV).

The list of details from Israel's covenant tradition could be lengthened, but the point seems adequately made that voluntary charity toward the poor and dispossessed was not enough. The entire social order was structured in a way that attempted to prevent those in need from being permanently locked into their poverty.

The economics of equality was also a part of the pattern of community in the early Christian church. In the book of Acts we find this report immediately following the Pentecost experience: "All who believed were together and had all things in common; and they sold their possessions and goods and distributed them to all, as any had need" (Acts 2:44–45; cf. also 4:32). Even more striking is Paul's letter to the church at Corinth concerning a collection he is taking up for the church in Jerusalem, which has fallen into severe economic difficulties. "I do not mean that others should be eased and you burdened, but that as a matter of equality your abundance at the present time should supply their want, so that their abundance may supply your want, that there may be equality. As it is written, 'He who gathered much had nothing over, and he who gathered little had no lack' "

(2 Cor. 8:13–15). Paul has returned to the principle of the manna story.

ON TO SINAI

The church in our time needs desperately to appropriate the images of Sinai as well as those of exodus. We must become involved in working for social structures that embody God's demand for justice and righteousness. The stress of Sinai is upon corporate as well as individual action. The call is for systemic care rather than for episodic concern. The crises facing this world with its limited resources and its great gap between the rich and powerful and the poor and powerless cannot be forestalled by Band-Aid responses to crises while the need for whole new structures of justice goes unnoticed. The biblical word is clear: We cannot seek our own salvation without seeking that of our neighbor, and we cannot minister to the anguish of our neighbor's soul without ministering to the suffering of our neighbor's body. We have been called into covenant by the action of a free God who has chosen caring relationship to this world. Exodus frees us from the forced labor that builds the pharaoh's cities, but Sinai calls us to the covenantal labor that is necessary to build the just community.

4

LIKE THE OTHER NATIONS

*   *   *

Israel's journey from the sacred mountain of Sinai led into the long years of the wilderness and toward the land of the promise. The wilderness was a place of paradox where in settings of hardship and trial Israel learned to trust in God's providence. "God . . . knows your going through this great wilderness; these forty years the Lord your God has been with you; you have lacked nothing" (Deut. 2:7). Ironically, it will be in the land of promise where hardship has seemingly been left behind that Israel will be most tempted to forget God's providence. The sojourner and the wanderer become the dweller and the possessor.

The land is an important Old Testament symbol, embodying both promise and danger for the people of God. Those who are summoned by God's call away from preoccupation with securing a place in the world are promised the gift of place through God's grace. For Israel that place was the land into which they came by crossing the Jordan River.

It is unfortunate that this experience of coming into the land is so frequently referred to in scholarly and church literature as "the conquest." The dominant witness in the Old Testament is to the land as a gift of grace, not as the spoils of violence. Much of the book of

Deuteronomy is a speech on the eve of entry, in which Moses stresses the character of the land as an opportunity to continue the receiving of life as God's gift. Much like Israel had learned to trust God's gift in the manna and quail of the wilderness, they were to trust that their needs would be provided for in the land to which God had brought them.

> For the Lord your God is bringing you into a good land, a land of brooks of water, of fountains and springs, flowing forth in valleys and hills, a land of wheat and barley, of vines and fig trees and pomegranates, a land of olive trees and honey, a land in which you will eat bread without scarcity, in which you will lack nothing, a land whose stones are iron, and out of whose hills you can dig copper. And you shall eat and be full, and you shall bless the Lord your God for the good land he has given you. (Deut. 8:7–10)

But the land is not just the gift of the promise. It is also the source of danger and temptation. Those called to receive are tempted to seize and grasp. What has come from God is claimed as human accomplishment.

Many of the most troublesome traditions of Joshua and Judges reflect the telling of Israel's story for this period from the perspective of those who gave in to the temptations of exclusivism, pride, and nationalism. The first eleven chapters of Joshua describe the entry into the land in terms of heroes and conquest in which all the Canaanites were destroyed (Josh. 10:40–43; 11:21–23). This was not historically the case. We know from later biblical stories that many Canaanite cities were scattered throughout Israel. We know from Joshua 12–24, where much detailed information on early Israelite settlement is recorded, that many tribes did not come into possession of their land by conquest.

The battle stories of Joshua and some portions of Judges reflect an attitude of "The only good Canaanite is a dead Canaanite." But this is not the dominant biblical attitude toward the gift of land. Exclusivism, pride, and nationalism are considered the dangers to avoid when land tempts Israel to forget its reliance on God's grace.

> Take heed lest you forget the Lord your God . . . lest when you have eaten and are full, and have built goodly houses and live in them . . . and all that you have is multiplied, then your heart be lifted up, and you forget the Lord your God, who brought you out of the land of Egypt . . . who led you through the great and terrible wilderness. . . . Beware lest you say in your heart, "My power and the might of my hand have gotten me this wealth." (Deut. 8:11–15, 17)

It was because of the temptations of land that Israel was called to remember exodus for the sake of humility in the face of God's grace. "You shall remember that you were a slave in the land of Egypt, and the Lord your God redeemed you" (Deut. 15:15). Unfortunately, the experience of Israel in the land is one which amply testifies to the dangers as well as the promise. It is to the story of Israel in the land that we turn.

Make Us a King

For almost two hundred years after settlement in the land (ca. 1225–1020 B.C.), Israel lived as a tribal federation. The period reflected in the book of Judges is one in which we can see glimpses of Israel attempting to live out its life in accordance with the covenantal understanding described in chapter 3. Although the tribes cooperated in maintaining a central sanctuary and a priesthood to serve it, they resisted the creation of centralized political structures and roles, maintaining a non-hierarchical system of tribal cooperation that tended more to grass-roots-up functioning.

The period of the Judges was not, however, an easy time. Threats from external enemies (e.g., the Midianites in Judges 6–8) and intertribal conflict (Judges 20) threatened the security and stability of the covenant league. In times of danger, leaders came to the fore to meet the crisis, and Israel's storytellers understood these "judges" (as they were called) to be agents of God's deliverance. Ideally all tribes would respond to give aid when any were threatened with danger. In practice, the response was often limited to the immediate area of the threat. Thus, even in the time of the Judges, some began to question the covenantal system for its lack of centralized political authority. In Judges 8:22–23, the men of Israel ask Gideon to become a king over them, and his sons to follow, but Gideon refuses, saying that only Yahweh is to rule over Israel. An earthly ruler is seen as a conflict with God's sovereignty. One of Gideon's sons tries to make himself king (Abimelech in Judges 9), but the attempt is abortive and Abimelech meets a tragic end.

It is clear from historical and archaeological evidence that the threat of the Philistines finally forced Israel to the establishment of kingship. The Philistines were a non-Semitic people who came from the sea and settled on the coastal plain about the same time that the Israelites were settling inland. They were an aggressive military-minded people with ambitions for a wider kingdom, and around 1050 B.C. they attacked the Israelites in an apparent effort to take over. Israel's loosely structured tribal organization proved unable to meet this concerted threat. In a disastrous series of reversals the nonprofessional Israelite troops were defeated, the ark of the covenant was captured, and the central sanctuary at Shiloh was destroyed (1 Samuel 4–6). Philistine garrisons were established throughout the land. Ironworking was made a Philistine monopoly (1 Sam. 13:19–23). Israel was on the verge of extinction.

It was the remarkable figure of Samuel, perhaps the first of the true prophets, who seems to have kept the traditions and identity of Israel alive in this crisis period (see 1 Samuel 1–15). It is he who acted as the agent of God in anointing Saul to be the first of Israel's kings to "save my people from the hand of the Philistines" (1 Sam. 9:16).

Kingship is not, however, seen in the biblical story as a purely positive development. Historians say kingship was made necessary by the Philistines, but theologically the scripture in its final form sees the people's request for a king as a sinful rejection of God's rule over them, a violation of covenant trust. When the people come to Samuel to ask for a king in 1 Samuel 8, they ask that they become "like all the [other] nations" (vs. 5, 20). They not only ask for the resources to meet the crisis but are willing to give up their alternative pattern of peoplehood for the sake of security. Israel's calling as a covenant people is threatened in an effort to seek the security of kingship because this is the way of other nations.

Saul becomes Israel's first king (1 Samuel 9–11). He is anointed by God's prophet Samuel as the chosen one, but the people are warned of the dangers kingship brings (1 Sam. 8:10–18). The king can serve Israel's covenant God, but the temptation will be great to give in to the desire to be "like the nations." Saul is a man caught between two worlds. He falls into conflict with Samuel and the covenant tradition as he tries to develop new patterns of royal institution (1 Sam. 13:8–15; 15:1–35). He is rejected by Samuel. He becomes a haunted and at times demented

man. As it becomes clear that David is to be God's choice
as Saul's successor, Saul becomes obsessed with jealousy.
Finally and tragically, Saul takes his own life after seeing
his army defeated by the Philistines and his son Jonathan
killed in the battle (1 Samuel 31). Kingship is now a
reality in Israel, but it has brought a tension into the
heart of Israel's faith. Can kingship serve the covenant
ideal? It remains for the reign of David and his son Solomon to show both the rich possibilities and the grave
dangers to Israel's faith.

ROYAL IDEAL AND ROYAL REALITY

In spite of the sinful desire to be like the nations,
kingship is viewed in much of the Old Testament tradition as capable of serving the covenant faith of Israel.
Prophets anointed the kings and held them accountable
to God's will. There developed a royal ideal of the
king as defender and champion of the covenant and its
God.

In Deuteronomy 17:14–20, the covenant-based law
code of the Deuteronomist includes a law of the king. It
provides that one from among the covenant community
("your brother") whom God chooses may become king
(v. 15), but the king is not to exploit his position by
accumulating horses, wives, or wealth (vs. 16–17). However, most important, "he shall write for himself in a
book a copy of this law . . . and it shall be with him, and
he shall read in it all the days of his life, that he may learn
to fear the Lord his God, by keeping all the words of this
law and these statutes, and doing them; that his heart
may not be lifted up above his brethren, and that he may
not turn aside from the commandment" (vs. 18–20). Thus
the royal ideal is of a king who is not a center of authority

unto himself but derives authority from the covenant law of God.

Such a hope for an ideal covenant king is richly reflected in royal psalms such as 72:

> Give the king thy justice, O God,
>   and thy righteousness to the royal son!
> May he judge thy people with righteousness,
>   and thy poor with justice! . . .
> May he defend the cause of the poor of the people,
>   give deliverance to the needy,
>   and crush the oppressor!
>
> (Psalm 72:1–2, 4)

This royal ideal is also the source of hope for an eschatological anointed one (messiah) who will someday establish God's kingdom of peace:

> There shall come forth a shoot from the stump of Jesse,
>   and a branch shall grow out of its roots . . .
> with righteousness he shall judge the poor,
>   and decide with equity for the meek of the earth;
> and he shall smite the earth with the rod of his mouth,
>   and with the breath of his lips he shall slay the wicked.
> Righteousness shall be the girdle of his waist,
>   and faithfulness the girdle of his loins.
>
> (Isaiah 11:1, 4–5)

In Israel's story it is David who first embodies this ideal. He is not pictured as an artificially perfect king (e.g., the well-known episode of his sin with Bathsheba in 2 Samuel 11–12), but he is seen as one who strove for faithfulness to the covenant and repented when called to account by the prophets. In later Israelite tradition, the name of David is used to represent the royal ideal. The importance of Jesus as the son of David in New Testament tradition points to Jesus' own claim to fulfill that royal ideal of the kingly figure as the servant of God's kingdom.

But if David represents the royal ideal and its faithful possibilities, his son Solomon brings into full view a royal reality which in practice produces kings who subvert the covenant for their own purposes of power and wealth. With Solomon we see the emergence of a royal pattern that is the enemy of the covenant pattern discussed in chapter 3. Even Israel's own historians in assessing the kings find only four who can be judged positively when measured by covenant standards. The history of kingship in Israel is largely a journey away from covenant which begins with Solomon.

The pattern of royal reality emerges first of all in the realm of economics. To replace the economics of equality, Solomon and subsequent kings introduced an *economics of privilege*. Privilege entered the picture as an outgrowth of the unprecedented affluence and well-being enjoyed by Israel in the Solomonic period. "Solomon's provision for one day was thirty cors of fine flour, and sixty cors of meal, ten fat oxen, and twenty pasture-fed cattle, a hundred sheep, besides harts, gazelles, roebucks, and fatted fowl" (1 Kings 4:22–23). This is hardly the provision of the average Israelite. For the first time on a large and continuous scale in Israel, resources were being distributed not on the basis of need but of privileged position.

In the previous periods of Israel's life the Mosaic covenant had governed the equitable distribution of scarce resources. Now, with abundant resources, distribution becomes increasingly unequal, with a privileged few enjoying a disproportionate share of the wealth. From this point onward a clear growth of radical class distinctions can be traced in Israel. King, royal court, nobility, and landowners formed the wealthy class at the top. Much more numerous and separated from the wealthy by a great economic and social gulf were the peasants of the land. By the time of Amos these class divisions had hardened. The classical prophets, beginning with Amos in the eighth century, direct a large portion of their message of judgment at those who profit, actively or passively, from economic exploitation (e.g., Amos 6:4–7; 8:4–6; Micah 2:1–2; Jer. 22:13–17).

The economics of privilege made necessary the replacement of a politics of justice with a *politics of oppression*. Listen to 1 Kings 5:13–14: "King Solomon raised a levy of forced labor out of all Israel; and the levy numbered thirty thousand men. And he sent them to Lebanon, ten thousand a month in relays; they would be a month in Lebanon and two months at home." Look also at 9:15: "And this is the account of the forced labor which King Solomon levied to build the house of the Lord and his own house."

Since the resources and benefits of Solomonic greatness were not shared equitably, royal power was introduced to maintain privilege and to deal with discontent. Although the use of forced labor is the most flagrant example, Solomon also used excessive and inequitable taxation, and he dismantled the tribal system of participatory governance. The tribal system was replaced with administrative districts, cutting across tribal lines and administered by governors appointed by and accountable to the king alone (1 Kings 4:7–19). The royal politics was hierarchical and authoritarian.

Evidence of growing discontent appears with the emergence for the first time of revolution within Israel because of the tyranny of its own king. First Kings 11:26–40 tells of an attempt at rebellion led by a young royal official named Jeroboam. Although his revolt fails, he escapes into Egypt and returns after the death of Solomon to lead the elders of the ten northern tribes in their demands for relief from oppression. Solomon's foolish son, Rehoboam, replies that he intends to be even more oppressive (1 Kings 12), and the northern kingdom splits off to form a nation apart from the southern tribe of Judah (the tribe of the Davidic kings). The unity of the covenant people is permanently divided as a result of the politics of oppression.

The politics of oppression continued to be a pattern of royal power. The period of monarchy was filled with the stories of flagrant greed and oppressive power used by the kings to subvert the intention of the Mosaic covenant for their own gain. The story of Naboth's vineyard and Elijah's confrontation of Ahab and Jezebel is a prime example (1 Kings 21). Some of Israel's kings, unlike Solomon or Ahab or Manasseh, are not flagrant in their misuse of power, but they do not act to restore or defend covenant equity and justice. The prophets are quite clear that the politics of oppression can express itself in managerial fashion as well as in overt shows of naked force (Amos 6:4–6). Oppression can be the oppression of disregard in a society that is divided along power and privilege lines.

The change in the economic and political patterns is accompanied by a change in the religious consciousness in Israel as well. An economics of privilege and a politics of oppression cannot coexist with the religion of a radically free God, especially if that God has already sided with the dispossessed and against the powerful, as in the exodus from Egypt. In place of the religion of God's radical freedom there begins in the Solomonic period the development of a *religion of God's domestication.* God ceases to be seen as radically free and is instead made institutionally accessible and subservient to nationalistic sentiment and privileged power.

The domestication of God in Israelite religion can be seen in two forms, idolatry and nationalistic religion. Idolatry is an obvious form of domestication of God. It limits and controls the presence of God by confining it to an object. To have the divine presence constantly available and dependent on human care was very tempting to Israel and its kings. King Solomon became a flagrant worshiper of idols and is judged very harshly for it in 1 Kings 11. Many of the subsequent kings allowed idolatry even to the extent of permitting idols in the temple in Jerusalem.

The temple itself became a chief symbol of nationalized religion. It was built with forced labor as part of Solomon's monumental building program. Access to God in the temple was controlled by a priesthood that itself served under the patronage of the king. Zadok and his family are installed as permanent hereditary priests of the Jerusalem temple. This choice is a reward to Zadok for his support of Solomon over Adonijah in the struggle for succession to David's throne (1 Kings 2). Thus the priesthood itself owes its position to the king's patronage.

The temple represents a religion of God's accessibility and domestication in a way not seen before in Israel. God is now said to dwell in the temple on Mount Zion in Jerusalem (Ps. 132:13–14). Access to God's presence was controlled by the priesthood and an elaborate sacrificial system. Regulations of cleanness and uncleanness, as well as necessary payments and sacrifices, begin to exclude some from the presence of God in the temple. Eventually priests and shrines outside of Jerusalem are declared illegitimate and closed (2 Kings 23:8–9).

In Judah the royal theology also included the notion that God had permanently blessed a single royal dynasty, the house of David (2 Sam. 8:16). As in Egypt and other ancient cultures, the favor of God is now linked to the fortunes of a particular national dynasty.

For the first time, Israel had a God who was in danger of being defined in nationalistic and institutional terms. The dangers of acculturated religion became reality in much of the period of the monarchy. Once again the prophets are forced to oppose this corruption of covenant, often by dangerously opposing the king himself or the temple. A classic example is Jeremiah's famous temple sermon in which he denounces those who cry "The temple of the Lord, the temple of the Lord, the temple of the Lord" as if the presence of the temple will magically relieve them of the consequences of national pride and arrogance or the responsibilities of covenant obedience (Jer. 7:1–4).

MESSENGERS TO THE NATION

Throughout our discussion of Israel's experience with kingship we have had occasion to mention the prophets. The role of the prophet from biblical times to the present has been the proclaiming of God's judgment and hope. To be a prophet is to be called by God to speak the divine Word. It is an audacious role. In the Old Testament this role was taken by individuals who seemed to function in a distinct office, although those who were prophets were drawn from widely different circumstances of life.

Prophets appear in the Bible at the same time as kingship, almost as if the dangers of kingship and nationhood required the prophets as guardians and champions of covenantal faith. They appear as the messengers of God, often speaking God's word in first-person oracles after the style of ancient messengers. "Thus saith the Lord" is a frequent beginning.

The early prophets appear as characters in the history of Israel in the books of Samuel and Kings. We know little of their message, but we see them courageously confronting covenant-breaking kings, opposing idolatry, and championing the worship of Yahweh. Some of these prophets are insiders in the royal court, yet they pronounce judgment even on the king when it is warranted (e.g., Nathan, in 2 Samuel 12). Others, such as Elijah, operate outside the royal structures, are often considered enemies rather than advisers of the king, and sometimes even risk their lives (1 Kings 18–19).

In the eighth century, the preaching of some individual prophets began to be preserved and passed on. This prophetic preaching has come down to us in the books of the Old Testament that bear the names of the prophets, and we refer to these as the classical prophets. Among them are Amos, Hosea, Isaiah, and Micah in the eighth century; Jeremiah in the period immediately preceding the Babylonian destruction of Jerusalem in 587; and Ezekiel and an anonymous prophet we call Second Isaiah who preached during the time of exile.

The prophetic literature is very rich, and much has been written about the prophets in modern times. We can only scratch the surface in this book, so we will confine comments to some general observations on the prophets and slight the richness of each prophet's individual message.

It is important to underline the prophetic task as the proclaiming of judgment *and* hope. The prophets are often pictured incorrectly as sayers of doom only. In reality, their prophetic message of hope is as rich as their message of judgment is jarring. Judgment and hope in the prophetic material are two sides of the same divine message. Judgment without hope is barren, and hope without judgment is hollow. In this chapter we focus on the theme of judgment. In the next chapter we will discuss prophetic hope because it comes so strongly to the fore in relation to the experience of exile.

Several aspects of prophetic judgment are noteworthy. First, the judgment that the prophet announces is always God's judgment. The prophet is a messenger, not simply a commentator. The prophets are steeped in the traditions of Israel's faith, so that discernment of what God is doing always takes place out of a consciousness of what God has done. Those in the modern church who would speak in prophetic judgment must do so only after carefully weighing their speaking against what we know of God through the tradition and experience of the community of faith. We must be careful not to lend the authority of God's name to our own opinions, however worthy, if we have not sought out their relationship to God's word.

Second, prophetic judgment is internal as well as external. The covenant community itself was the recipient of prophetic judgment, not just its external enemies. Israel often failed to understand this and turned against prophets who dared to speak the truth about the covenant disobedience of their own people. Amos' oracles against the nations end by including among them an oracle against Israel as well (Amos 1–2). Whatever opposes God's intention for the world and creates brokenness is deserving of God's judgment. The community of faith when it participates in brokenness is especially judged because it is charged with the missional task of enabling and promoting justice and wholeness. The implication for the modern church is that we cannot simply point to the brokenness of the world but must confront the brokenness of our own lives and communities.

Finally, we can briefly summarize the content of the prophetic message of judgment as an indictment of self-interest, self-righteousness, and self-delusion.

The prophets constantly point to the abuses that come from the placing of one's self-interest above the interests of all others, even to the extent of exploiting the weaker members of the society. Social class consciousness, economic exploitation, judicial corruption, political oppression, and exclusivism are all condemned by the prophets as antithetical to God's desire for full life and wholeness for all (Amos 2:6–8; Isa. 5:1–10; 58:3–7; Hos. 4:1–3).

It is the covenant qualities of justice and righteousness that are to guide the community of faith away from self-interested action. The Hebrew word for justice *(mishpat)* can be translated as either justice or judgment. It is the seeking after full integrity for the life of every person. It acts as the advocate of those in need of support (justice) and confronts those who would exploit others to their own advantage (judgment). Thus, justice in the prophetic meaning is pastoral and confrontational at the same time. If the prophet's words seem harsh to the privileged, they must seem as music to the dispossessed. Righteousness *(tsedaqah)* points to the relational quality of covenant obedience. One achieves righteousness not by obeying some abstract standard or set of rules (see the story of Tamar in Genesis 38 where she is pronounced righteous), but by caring for the welfare of those with whom we are in relationship, seeking their wholeness and integrity.

It is when the qualities of justice and righteousness are absent that Israel's worship becomes self-righteous and hypocritical. Pious religious observance without concern for the neighbor becomes blasphemous in the eyes of God. Religious relationship to God in worship and prayer is not possible apart from God's mission to heal a broken world.

> I hate, I despise your feasts,
>   and I take no delight in your solemn assemblies.
> Even though you offer me your burnt offerings and cereal offerings,
>   I will not accept them . . .
> Take away from me the noise of your songs;
>   to the melody of your harps I will not listen.
> But let justice roll down like waters,
>   and righteousness like an ever-flowing stream.
>   (Amos 5:21–24)

Equally false is the worship of idols, for it reduces God to a thing that can be controlled, and the purpose is usually the materialistic seeking of guarantees for the fertility and richness of the land. "My people inquire of a thing of wood, and their staff gives them oracles" (Hos. 4:12).

Less commonly observed, the prophets also had a word of judgment for two forms of self-delusion. On the one hand are those who because they have not explicitly exploited the poor and the weak imagine themselves without guilt or responsibility. But to the prophets, those who stand by and do nothing are held equally accountable. "Woe to those who lie upon beds of ivory, and stretch themselves upon their couches, and eat lambs from the flock, and calves from the midst of the stall; who sing idle songs to the sound of the harp . . . but are not grieved over the ruin of Joseph!" (Amos 6:4–6).

Another form of self-delusion is that indulged in by those who simply fail to acknowledge the brokenness of their world. They proclaim things to be fine while thousands of suffering faces become invisible around them. It seems to be the kings and others in positions of authority who are most often singled out for prophetic words on this matter, such as this passage from Jeremiah 6:14: "They have healed the wound of my people lightly, saying, 'Peace, peace,' when there is no peace."

The prophetic preaching not only judges but calls hearers to repentance and restoration of covenant obedience. Perhaps no better summary verse could be found than that of Micah 6:8 which gives the title to this book: "What does the Lord require of you but to do justice, and to love kindness, and to walk humbly with your God?"

5

BY THE WATERS
OF BABYLON

❋ ❋ ❋

Just as the central event in Israel's early story was the
exodus experience, the latter part of Israel's story is
dominated by the experience of Babylonian exile. Exodus comes out of the experience of oppression and dis-
possession, but exile reflects the tragic results of Israel's
attempts to manipulate the blessings and to overturn the
covenant. In both exodus and exile, God's grace has a
further word to say, but it takes a different shape in the
midst of the judgment of exile. It is to the shape of hope
in the midst of judgment that we turn our attention in
this chapter.

The path to exile is one in which the call to covenant
obedience is constantly weakened or displaced by the
temptations of the royal model we discussed earlier. Idolatry and nationalized religion challenge and attempt to
control the Yahweh-centered faith of covenant. Justice
and righteousness are not served in the relations of
neighbor to neighbor. The gulf between wealthy and
poor has grown great. Worship of the covenant God in
the face of these realities has become hypocrisy.

As we have seen, it was the great classical prophets
who confronted Israel in these matters and championed
the covenant way. The great prophet of the period leading up to the exile was Jeremiah. His preaching began in

626 and only ended after Jerusalem was destroyed in 587
B.C.

In his early ministry, Jeremiah spoke of God's judgment on idolatry and lack of covenant justice in a manner
similar to earlier prophets. But in 621 an unusual thing
happened. A lawbook was discovered during repairs on
the temple, and on hearing its words the young king,
Josiah, launched an extensive covenant renewal program
(2 Kings 22–23). That lawbook was the book of
Deuteronomy, a collection of sermons and laws spelling
out the covenant understanding and its implementation
in terms appropriate to the time of Jeremiah and Josiah.
Many of its passages are still among the clearest statements of the demands that covenant makes on God's
people: "Hear, O Israel: The Lord our God is one Lord;
and you shall love the Lord your God with all your heart,
and with all your soul, and with all your might" (Deut.
6:4–5).

For a brief time under Josiah there is the possibility of
a renewed, covenant-shaped Israel, but Josiah is killed in
battle in 609 B.C. His covenant reforms do not outlast
him, because he is succeeded by shortsighted and greedy
kings. Jeremiah feels forced to take up his preaching
again and to denounce the patterns of idolatry, injustice,
and national arrogance that have reasserted themselves.

Increasingly, Jeremiah sees the possibility of disaster
in the form of conquest and exile as the potential judgment on Israel's sin. He denounces those who cry
" 'Peace, peace,' when there is no peace" (Jer. 6:14; 8:11),
refusing to recognize the dangers. He preaches against
those who seem to feel some special privileged protection
because Jerusalem has the temple of the Lord, as if God
were the possession of Israel (Jeremiah 7).

It is in the book of Jeremiah that we see the anguish

of prophetic preaching. In Jeremiah's confessions (e.g., 15:10–21; 17:14–18; 20:7–18) we see the pain of Jeremiah in bringing the message of judgment that he feels compelled to bring. To speak the confronting Word of God can never be a matter of glib self-righteousness. It is because Jeremiah loves and identifies with Israel that his preaching of judgment is both necessary and painful.

Unfortunately, the kings and leaders of Jeremiah's time embarked on policies of national pride that assumed God would protect them from the consequences. It was not to be so. In 597 B.C. a Babylonian army laid siege to Jerusalem. Jerusalem surrendered, and a first group of exiles were taken away to Babylon.

THE MEANING OF EXILE

In 587 B.C., when the leaders of Jerusalem were convinced God would restore the nation to its deserved greatness, the Babylonian army was forced to return. This time the Babylonians were not inclined to mercy. It broke through the walls of Jerusalem, destroyed the temple, reduced the city to rubble, and carried all prominent citizens of the kingdom into exile (2 Kings 25). It would be hard to overstate the devastating impact of this catastrophe. Modern readers tend to think of Babylonian exile mainly in terms of geography, but for Israel exile was *a cultural, political, and religious upheaval.* All those centers of meaning Israel had thought secure were overturned. Exile was a calling into question of Israel's way of life, its institutions of leadership, and even its faith. The prosperity many thought of as birthright was destroyed, the Davidic kingship ended, and the temple was in ruins.

Needless to say, the mood of the exile reflected not

only the pain of physical suffering but the hopelessness of despair and anger. Psalm 137 best captures this mood:

> By the waters of Babylon,
>   there we sat down and wept,
>   when we remembered Zion.
> On the willows there
>   we hung up our lyres.
> For there our captors
>   required of us songs,
> and our tormentors, mirth, saying,
>   "Sing us one of the songs of Zion!"
> (vs. 1–3, RSV)

> How shall we sing the Lord's song
>   in a strange land?
> (v. 4, KJV)

The implied answer to the psalmist's question is that they cannot sing the Lord's song. Indeed, many thought God had abandoned them (Lam. 5:19–22).

God had not abandoned Israel, but the prophets were all agreed that God had judged Israel. "Who gave up Jacob to the spoiler, and Israel to the robbers? Was it not the Lord, against whom we have sinned, in whose ways they would not walk, and whose law they would not obey?" (Isa. 42:24). God had not willfully forsaken Israel. The catastrophe was related to Israel's own arrogance, injustice, and unfaithfulness. God judged such sin even in God's own people. They had no special privilege or immunity.

The modern church has not often chosen to think of itself in terms of the exile image. This is partly because we limit our understanding of exile to the geographic. The fate of the Israelite exiles seems to us a happening possible only in ancient times and therefore treated as irrelevant.

But even when we understand exile more broadly as an upheaval in the whole community's pattern of living and meaning we still find the theme of judgment experienced as catastrophe a hard one to consider. No one wishes to believe that catastrophic experiences will befall them, and even fewer wish to believe that their own behavior has helped bring such a fate upon them. On first glance the theme of exile seems like such a negative one.

Nevertheless, we do live in a time that carries with it the possibility of cultural, political, and religious upheaval. Cherished patterns of living and structures of meaning have been and will be overturned.

We live in a time when famine, nuclear war, and major environmental damage are all disasters that are possible in our lifetimes. We live on a planet increasingly over-populated, and on which many of those peoples who have lived in poverty are asking for a just economic share in the earth's wealth. There are increasing signs that the unlimited consumption and general prosperity enjoyed by most Americans will not be possible in an increasingly limited world. Changes in our way of life will in turn challenge our values and priorities. Indeed, the rapid rate of change itself confuses us and alters our values. In such a world it is very likely that we shall go through upheavals that challenge our accepted patterns of life, meaning, and faith.

In effect, we too face the possibility of exile. Ours will not be a geographic removal, but it will be a strange land unlike that we have known—the strange land of our own future.

We have not raised the image of exile just to sound a gloomy note. Precisely the opposite! It is in the context of exile that we find biblical resources for moving from despair, resignation, and guilt to hope and renewal. If our time shares much in common with the period of Israel's exile, then the central question for the church today may also be the question of the psalmist, "How shall we sing the Lord's song in a strange land?" How can God's word be understood in a time when our accustomed way of life is coming apart?

This was the central question which occupied the great prophets of the exile when that catastrophe became reality. It has always been remarkable that the boldest messages of hope in the Old Testament come from that time of greatest hopelessness among the people, the Babylonian exile. After the destruction of Jerusalem, Jeremiah turned his preaching to themes of comfort and hope for a new covenant (Jeremiah 31). Ezekiel, carried off in the first deportation, spoke of God's presence with the people even in Babylon (Ezekiel 1) and new life in dry bones (Ezekiel 37). An anonymous prophet of the exile whom we call only Second Isaiah (Isaiah 40–55) sang the most eloquent hymns of hope contained in the Old Testament, "Comfort ye, comfort ye my people, saith your God" (Isa. 40:1, KJV).

SINGING THE LORD'S SONG

In scripture, judgment never stands alone but is coupled with hope. Likewise, hope in the Bible is often born out of situations where those without the eyes of faith might see only hopelessness. What enabled the prophets of the exile to sing the Lord's song when those around them were mired in despair? When their own present seemed so dismal, what made them confident of God's future?

Biblical hope is not founded in rational assessment of options. It is instead the confidence that even when all the options seem disastrous, the last word has not been spoken, for it comes from God. Here we can only comment on some of the forms of hope suggested in the biblical witness. They may provide some guide for the forms of hope the church might seek in our own time.

1. *Hope as Memory*. The community of faith has always been a community of hope because it is never left with just its own present resources. Over and over again in hopeless situations, the Old Testament writers called on images out of the past that called forth trust that the future also belonged to God. The Brazilian theologian Rubem Alves reminds us that "in the Biblical world, one hopes for the future because one has already seen the creative event taking place in the past."

Second Isaiah called upon the images of exodus and creation, joining them together as the work of the same God who delivers and orders, and proclaiming "new exodus" and "new creation." Jeremiah and Ezekiel both spoke of "new covenants of the heart." The early church proclaimed the hope of the resurrection as "new creation," the fulfillment of the promise to Abraham as "new covenant," and "a passing through the waters to new life" (exodus in the baptism imagery).

> Look to the rock from which you were hewn,
>   and to the quarry from which you were digged.
> Look to Abraham your father
>   and to Sarah who bore you.
>   (Isaiah 51:1–2)

Over and over again the community of faith draws hope from its memory of God's work. In this form, hope is *the antidote to rootlessness*. Memory protects the church from that lack of identity which tempts it simply to take on the coloration of its cultural surroundings (the chameleon church), just as many in hopelessness were swallowed up in the Babylonian surroundings of exile. The church must be wary that memory does not grow dim and hope thus remain formless in our time.

2. *Hope as Posterity.* In the Old Testament, hope was not narrowly limited to the benefits one desired in the scope of a lifetime. Biblical hope is the ability to see that God's future stretches beyond one's own generation. It is particularly important in the age of the "here-and-now generation" to recover this important biblical vision. Many have despaired at the inability of this generation to look beyond its immediate self-interest to make decisions that lay the foundations for peace and well-being of generations yet unborn. The church might do well to explore its own tradition for resources at this point. In Jeremiah's letter to the exiles, he wrote:

> Thus says the Lord of hosts, the God of Israel, to all the exiles whom I have sent into exile from Jerusalem to Babylon: Build houses and live in them; plant gardens and eat their produce. Take wives and have sons and daughters. . . . When seventy years are completed for Babylon, I will visit you, and I will fulfil to you my promise and bring you back to this place. (Jer. 29:4–6, 10)

Jeremiah was advising these exiles that hope would not reach full fruition in their own lifetime. Their hope lay in part in future generations for whom they must now live faithfully. For the most part, the Hebrews rejected the notion of individual immortality in favor of a concept of corporate posterity. The goal of faithful life was the furtherance of faithful generations to come after, not the achievement of individual reward in the life to come. Covenant included solidarity with the past experience of the community and responsibility for future generations.

For the church in our own time, recovery of this aspect of hope would *cut against excessive individualism,* which measures the impact of ethical decisions only on one's own life or, at the broadest, on one's own nation. The church must work to construct a concept of hope that looks beyond self-interest to allow faithful decisions which include advocacy of our own descendants.

3. *Hope as Forgiveness.* When we acknowledge and confess our own judgment, we can then hear the word of God's forgiveness. Second Isaiah opens his great hymn of hope: "Comfort, comfort my people, says your God. Speak tenderly to Jerusalem, and cry to her that her warfare is ended, that her iniquity is pardoned, that she has received from the Lord's hand double for all her sins" (Isa. 40:1–2). Hope springs from the knowledge that we are forgiven and loved by God in spite of our failures to serve the divine will. Those in Babylonian exile need more than the grace of God's deliverance (as in exodus from Egyptian bondage); they need also the grace of God's forgiveness.

It is hope as forgiveness that *frees us from guilt.* Many who realize that we (in our church and in our society) have contributed to the brokenness of our world are paralyzed by guilt or forced to deny our complicity in order to escape guilt. Judgment does not call for guilt but for repentance. Guilt is oriented to the past and paralyzes persons in regret for things that cannot be changed. The Hebrew word for repent is *shub,* which means "to turn around." It points to a changing of direction and to new, creative action. Repentance is oriented to the future as an alternative to the past, and it empowers new response. God's forgiveness frees from guilt, but it calls to repentance. The church in our time must learn from the experience of exile that it cannot afford to be paralyzed by guilt when it should be witnessing to God's forgiveness, which has already made creative response possible.

4. *Hope as New Creation and New Life.* In contrast to the upheavals and confusion that often accompany the experience of judgment and exile, hope has a joyful and affirming character. In this aspect, hope is the word that *drives out resignation and despair.* In the crisis of judgment, defeat seems total. The task of the church as the community of hope is like that of the prophets of exile to declare paradoxically that very same moment of apparent defeat as one of new creation and rebirth to new life.

> Have you not known? Have you not heard?
> The Lord is the everlasting God,
>   the Creator of the ends of the earth.
> He does not faint or grow weary,
>   his understanding is unsearchable.
> He gives power to the faint,
>   and to him who has no might he increases strength. . . .
> But they who wait for the Lord
>   shall renew their strength,
>   they shall mount up with wings like eagles,
> they shall run and not be weary,
>   they shall walk and not faint.
>
> (Isaiah 40:28–29, 31)

What does it mean to "wait for the Lord"? From what quarter will this new strength come? Basically, the community of faith is to be constantly alert to creative and life-giving possibility, even in chaotic and death-dealing situations. It is there that God's hopeful activity is to be found, and there that we are to join it. This may take us into some surprising places. Second Isaiah declared to the exiles that the instrument of God's salvation, God's anointed one (Hebrew: messiah), was Cyrus, the pagan king of Persia (Isa. 45:1–6). This must have been a shock to his hearers. But the prophet reminded them that our God is free and sovereign over all history. Like the exiles, the modern church if it serves such a God of all history must scan the horizon, alert to the hopeful presence of God wherever it may be found, and we can be certain that it will not always be in institutionally approved settings.

In our time both chaos and death, the opponents of creation and life, work their power. Chaos appears as that confusion, anxiety, and disorder which paralyzes action. Death is that sense of separation, alienation, and brokenness which leads to resignation and despair. But the biblical message of hope is that God constantly defeats both chaos and death to make available to us new creation and new life. The life-style of the community of hope is one characterized by the mood of Habakkuk 3:17–18:

> Though the fig tree do not blossom,
>   nor fruit be on the vines,
> the produce of the olive fail
>   and the fields yield no food,
> the flock be cut off from the fold
>   and there be no herd in the stalls,
> yet I will rejoice in the Lord,
>   I will joy in the God of my salvation.

5. *Hope as Eschatological Vision.* Biblical hope is not encompassed in the planning of programs, strategies, and evaluations. These are surely necessary in the church's response to the challenges of our broken world, but if

these activities are not fired by the vision of God's future
in its fullness, they will be in vain. There is an element
of hope that is *not* practical in any immediate sense.
God's people were always those fired with a vision impossible of earthly achievement, and they knew it. The
future, whatever their efforts, was God's. In the Old
Testament this vision is richly encompassed in the eschatological visions, which inspired faithful labor in the
present (even in exile) by revealing the fullness of God's
future.

> For you shall go out in joy,
>   and be led forth in peace;
> the mountains and the hills before you
>   shall break forth into singing,
>   and all the trees of the field shall clap their hands.
>   (Isaiah 55:12)

> They shall beat their swords into plowshares,
>   and their spears into pruning hooks;
> nation shall not lift up sword against nation,
>   neither shall they learn war any more.
>   (Isaiah 2:4)

This visionary aspect of hope is *the remedy for the narrow
pragmatism* that often afflicts church response to great
issues. As with all human institutions, the church is
afflicted with the desire for institutional success. But as
God's faithful community we are called to labor on behalf of a vision that is impossible and foolhardy by
human standards. We are called to live as witnesses and
agents of God's future.

Rootlessness, individualism, guilt, resignation, despair, and narrow pragmatism—these are the enemies of
hope. They were present in the midst of Babylonian

exile; they are present in the church today. But as the prophets discovered, we are not without resources in the richness of our biblical faith. It requires only the decision to declare our commitment to the task of becoming communities of hope who can sing the Lord's song as faithfully as did Jeremiah, Ezekiel, and Second Isaiah.

Behold My Servant

One final theme out of the exile experience must be touched upon. In the preaching of Second Isaiah are found four passages that witness to a figure called "the servant of the Lord." These servant songs (Isa. 42:1–4; 49:1–6; 50:4–9; 52:13—53:12) give us a new image for faithfulness to God's calling. In the image of servant, Israel was summoned to new understandings of its vocation and its suffering, the early church found a way to understand the messiahship of one whose kingdom was established through suffering and death, and we are called to new tasks as the servant church, willing to lose our life in order to save it.

Much has been written on the servant songs. We can do little more here than to suggest their richness and urge their study as a model for the life-style of the church in our own time. We will only comment briefly on the mission of the servant, the scope of this mission, and the life-style of servanthood.

The *mission* of the servant is to establish justice. Three times in the first servant song this is made clear: "he will bring forth justice to the nations" (42:1). The servant's mission thus reflects the twofold nature of the covenantal word justice *(mishpat)*. To those who look to God for help, justice brings hope, but to those who resist and oppose God's rule, justice becomes judgment and confrontation. The servant is to be the instrument of God's justice.

The *scope* of the servant's mission is universal. It is not simply directed to Israel but to the nations, the ends of the earth. This is made especially clear in the second servant song: "It is too light a thing that you should be my servant to raise up the tribes of Jacob and to restore the preserved of Israel; I will give you as a light to the nations, that my salvation may reach to the end of the earth" (49:6). The servant's task is not to a narrow confessing group but to all peoples.

Finally, the *life-style* of the servant is one of willingness to suffer for the sake of the mission. The way of servanthood will not be the way of earthly power ("a bruised reed he will not break," 42:3). The mission will lead him to be abused and scorned (50:4–9), but, as the fourth servant song makes especially clear, it is the servant's willing suffering that is redemptive. "He was wounded for our transgressions, he was bruised for our iniquities; upon him was the chastisement that made us whole [*shalom*], and with his stripes we are healed" (53:5). This picture of the servant is an Old Testament witness to the paradox of the gospel of weakness and suffering become power and victory. It is little wonder that the New Testament community saw in Jesus Christ the fullest expression of this servant role. But in the prophet's time these servant songs were already summoning the community to servanthood as a faithful response to God's word, and they live anew in addressing us with the call to become the servant church.

6

SAGES, VISIONARIES, AND POETS

* * *

In the Hebrew Bible the third section of the canon, alongside the Law and the Prophets, is called the Writings. This is a truly miscellaneous collection of witnesses. It ranges from the magnificent poetry of the Psalms and the Song of Songs to the strange visions of Daniel; from the assurance of Proverbs to the protest of Job; from the concern for Jewish identity in Ezra and Nehemiah to the universalism of Ruth and Jonah.

Virtually all the Writings received their final literary shape after the Babylonian exile (587–539 B.C.), although some, like the book of Psalms, are postexilic collections of materials that come from Israel's earlier life. For the most part the diversity of literature and viewpoint reflected in the Writings give us a picture of the postexilic period in Israel's story as characterized by great pluralism. Before the catastrophe of exile, most saw history as the arena of God's working, either in covenant or in kingship. God's salvation history was unfolding in the midst of Israel's story. Exile undermined confidence in God's working in history. Although the prophets of the exile (Jeremiah, Ezekiel, Second Isaiah) reaffirmed God's sovereign presence, it should not surprise us that following the exile some alternative perspectives for understanding God's relationship to Israel and to history should emerge. The diversity of the Writings witnesses to the differing theological options that drew interest in this last period of the Old Testament story. How should our relationship to God now be understood? There was more than one postexilic answer to this important question. Since it is often said that we too live in a pluralistic age, it may be that we can discover some clues in the Writings to weigh the competing claims that differing faith perspectives make on us today.

It will not be possible in the scope of this chapter to discuss every book in the Writings. We will attempt to examine three main perspectives within the postexilic witnesses and to show how many of the Old Testament books contained in the Writings fit within those perspectives.

RETURN AND RESTORATION

In 538 B.C., Cyrus, the king of the Medes and the Persians, entered Babylon, bringing its empire to an end. As already anticipated by the prophet of the exile we call Second Isaiah (45:1), Cyrus issued an edict (Ezra 1:2–4; 6:2–5) allowing the Jews to return to Jerusalem and to rebuild the temple. This was in keeping with his general policy of autonomy for subject peoples and respect for their religions.

Many did not avail themselves of this opportunity to return, and Jews remained dispersed throughout many lands of the ancient world. Ezra 2:64 says that 42,360 persons returned in the first caravan, led by a governor named Sheshbazzar. Judah was to be reestablished as a province in the Persian Empire.

The hardships facing this returned group were formidable. Jerusalem and the temple were still in rubble.

Among those descendants of Judeans left behind at the time of the exile, no strong religious identity had remained; they had intermixed with surrounding cultures in marriage and religious practice. The returnees, by contrast, had developed a strong bond of community centered on maintaining certain religious practices and identity. Tensions developed quickly and included opposition to the plans of the returnees by ruling authorities in Samaria and Ammon. The Samaritans, descendants of the settlers brought by Assyria into the northern kingdom when it was conquered in 721 B.C., and the Ammonites had enjoyed essential control over the territory of northern Judah (Edom controlled the south) until Cyrus by his edict reestablished a new province of Judah. Naturally hostilities broke out. Early plans to rebuild the temple bogged down, and the returnees were demoralized by the problems and pressures of building a restored community. Three periods of strong leadership in the restoration period enabled the community to survive and reestablish itself. The sources for this period are the books of Ezra and Nehemiah and the prophetic books of Haggai, Zechariah, and Malachi.

Under the leadership of Zerubbabel, a new governor and leader of a second group of returnees, and Jeshua, a priest, work was begun on rebuilding the temple in 520. With the encouragement of the prophets Haggai and Zechariah, and in spite of serious opposition from the Samaritans, the temple was completed and rededicated in 515 (Ezra 3–6). This was a considerable achievement and raised great hopes among the returned Jews. There is some indication that Zerubbabel was related to the line of David, and many may have hoped to see the restoration of the Davidic kingship and the rebirth of the nation. This was not to be. Zerubbabel disappears from the story (recalled, perhaps), and the focus of restored Israel becomes temple/priesthood/religious identity rather than kingship/national identity.

Already during the exile, new vigor in the priestly vision of Israel's future had appeared. Ezekiel's vision of a New Jerusalem (Ezekiel 40–48) included a restored temple as the focus of Israel's life and the priesthood as its chief leadership. Portions of the Pentateuch (Genesis through Deuteronomy) written during this period, as well as the history work of the Chronicler, reflect this new vigor of priestly leadership. At the risk of oversimplification, it would seem that for many in the restored community of Jerusalem the response to the challenge of exile was to turn attention away from king and nation and to focus Israel's identity on its religious life, centered around the temple and such common religious practices as the observance of the Sabbath. By the time of Malachi (460–450), the role of the prophet is almost entirely concerned with priestly and cultic matters; after Malachi's preaching, prophecy as a distinct role in Israel disappears entirely from view.

Nehemiah, a Jewish official in the court of the Persian king, received an appointment as governor of Judah and returned to give leadership in establishing the security of the Jerusalem community. Work at restoring the city and its walls had been forced to a standstill by the hostility of the Samaritans. Nehemiah organized an intensive work schedule, which completed and dedicated the walls of Jerusalem in 443 b.c. With a new sense of security from external threats, Nehemiah turned his attention to the internal community. In a series of reforms he sought to establish the identity and purity of the Jews by outlawing marriage to foreigners, urging strict observance of religious and Sabbath practices, and demanding stricter purity in temple worship, including the exclusion of foreign influences in the temple.

Nehemiah probably made two trips to Jerusalem to provide leadership, and he was followed by the arrival of Ezra, "a scribe skilled in the law of Moses" (Ezra 7:6). (The dating of Ezra's visit is difficult. Some would say late fifth century and others early fourth century B.C.) Ezra brought with him a book of the laws of Moses, which was read and interpreted to the people in a great assembly (Nehemiah 8). This became the basis for the renewal of Jewish faith and practice based on the law of Moses. Most scholars believe that Ezra's lawbook is to be understood as the first appearance of the Pentateuch as a completed written document put forward as a foundation and authority for Jewish faith and practice. Written scripture as an authority in the community was established by Ezra's reading, teaching, and interpreting. Like Nehemiah before him, Ezra urged purity of religious practice and social community in conformity with the laws of Moses. This once again included a purging of foreign influences, especially the dissolving of marriages to foreigners.

In this brief treatment of a complex period we can see an important danger emerging, a danger often present in the history of the church as well. In a period where survival of the community of faith seemed at stake, the leaders of the Jews chose to preserve the identity of the Jews and their security at the risk of exclusivism. There is a genuine danger here that the tradition will turn in upon itself and away from the world. It is a tendency often seen in the church when its institutional security seems threatened. We should not be too harsh in our judgment on this period of Israel's story. The dangers in this period were great. The Jews could have been swallowed up and their identity forever lost. But even in the Old Testament, there seems to be the judgment that in an effort to save itself the Jerusalemite community went too far in an exclusivist direction. Two small books contained in the Writings, Ruth and Jonah, are stories told during this period in a manner that protests the exclusivism of Nehemiah and Ezra.

Ruth, a story set in the time of the Judges, is a story of the courage of women. Against the odds of physical hardship and social custom, Ruth and Naomi find a way from death to life. Ruth, seen in the story as courageous and resourceful, is an unlikely heroine, for she is a Moabite woman. Yet this Moabite woman not only makes possible her own future but in Ruth 4:17 is revealed to be the great-grandmother of David, the greatest of Israel's kings.

Jonah is the story of a reluctant prophet sent to preach God's judgment to the people of Nineveh. He tries to escape God's commission but cannot. But when he preaches to the wicked people of Nineveh, to his shock they repent. To his utter dismay, God then relents and revokes the judgment. Jonah is then rebuked for his inability to see God as capable of mercy to all peoples, even Ninevites. Jonah's God is a universal God, caring for all peoples.

Jewish exclusivism in this restoration period may be understandable, but it is not acceptable. The God of Israel is much larger than that.

By Wisdom God Founded the Earth

Contained in the Writings are a number of books commonly described as the Wisdom literature. These are Proverbs, Job, and Ecclesiastes. In addition there are two wisdom books in the apocrypha, Ben Sirach and Wisdom of Solomon, and scholars have more recently detected the influence of a wisdom perspective on other portions of the Old Testament, such as the Joseph stories, some of the material on David, prophets like Amos and Isaiah, and a handful of wisdom psalms (e.g., 16; 37; 49).

The beginnings of a wisdom tradition in Israel lie as early as King Solomon. It is an international tradition. Egypt and Babylon also have literature that reflects upon and teaches about the common concern for meaning in human life. These traditions are passed on in the teachings of sages and preserved in collections of proverbs and reflections on what makes for wisdom rather than folly. Israel's Wisdom literature has clearly borrowed from and been influenced by this international tradition.

Yet despite the early appearance of sages and wise teachings in Israel, all the wisdom books are from postexilic times. It would seem that wisdom enjoyed a new popularity, appealing to a broader audience (early wisdom was probably found mainly in the royal court), in the period after the exile. Much of this can be understood as a reaction to the failure of salvation history. The notion that God is active in the great events of history seeking the redemption of the world (and of Israel) was called into question by the catastrophe of exile. Wisdom has no concern for the drama of salvation in history. There is no mention of exodus, covenant, kingship, or prophets and little mention of temple or priests or sacrifices. The concerns of wisdom are matters of ordinary life and how one is to be wise rather than foolish in the conduct of daily affairs. The stress is on individual life rather than on the life of peoples. How appealing this down-to-earth context must have seemed to those scarred by exile!

Particularly in the book of Proverbs, the most representative of the wisdom books, we can see several emphases that deserve highlighting as characteristic of the wisdom perspective.

First, God appears in wisdom only as Creator and Sustainer rather than as Deliverer, Covenant-maker, or Judge. The presence of God is as order and not as act. This is a return to the God who blesses rather than the God who saves. Creation provides for the orderly parameters in which human existence is lived out. Salvation (wisdom) is found as people recognize and actualize the potential for wholeness already inherent in the created order. Emphasis is placed on the continuity of God's presence in creation rather than on the discontinuity of divine intervention in history. Our attention is diverted from the hope for God's redemptive intervention to the effort to discern the wise order which God intended as the arena for human existence. In a sense, human striving after wisdom aligns us with God's purposes in creation, since God "by wisdom" created the earth (Prov. 3:19).

Second, within the order of creation the purpose of human existence is life. Whatever does not contribute to bringing life is characterized as death. Life is intrinsic in the created order and needs only to become actualized in its fullness for each individual. Hence, the emphasis in wisdom is often on what seem like mundane matters. The wholeness *(shalom)* of human existence is already present as the promise of God's blessing on those who seek life.

In salvation history, existence is given its center of meaning by the intervention of God in a particular history. In the hands of a prosperous people, whether ancient Israel or modern America, this notion can foster a concept of election that claims a corner on God's presence. Wisdom, on the other hand, stresses seeking after life as seeking after the welfare of the whole human community to which one is related. The path of wisdom is pursued by individuals, but the concern is the whole community. "When it goes well with the righteous, the city rejoices" (Prov. 11:10). This aspect of wisdom obviously helps provide a corrective to the dangers of exclusivism and triumphalism seen in Nehemiah and Ezra.

Third, great importance is placed on human freedom and responsibility in the Wisdom literature. Persons are accorded a greater role in determining their own destiny. A central role is given to the notion that persons have choices to make. Each must decide responsibly by choosing life or death. If one chooses foolishly rather than wisely, one must bear the consequences of that choice, but it is by no means assumed that a person is destined always to make the sinful choice. The salvation history, symbolized by the exodus event, stresses our powerlessness and inability to effect a change in the human situation and, therefore, the need for God's deliverance. Wisdom does not arise out of the experience of powerlessness; it emphasizes the trust God has placed in human creatures and their responsibility and capacity to make decisions that will bring life and blessing in the created order.

There are limits to human potential, and persons are called upon to acknowledge their creaturely status. The limits are defined by the order of creation. To attempt to transcend those limits and become "like God" (Gen. 3:5) is to violate God's creation. God is present in the potential for life and wisdom as Creator and Sustainer and present in the limits of creation, exacting the consequences of sinful and foolish choices. There are limits to human capacity, but within those limits persons are not incapacitated, and much is expected of them. Such a biblical understanding provides a more fruitful base for reflecting on the uses of power than does a sole stress on salvation history, with its emphasis on human powerlessness.

Up to this point we have been stressing the positive contributions of the wisdom tradition. There are some dangers inherent in the wisdom perspective that can be seen especially in the book of Proverbs. Wisdom and folly are equated with righteousness and wickedness. It is assumed that these qualities are rewarded or punished in material terms. Thus, the righteous (wise) prosper and the wicked (foolish) perish. In Proverbs it almost seems that there is a mechanical cosmos designed to mete out rewards and punishments by tallying up one's wisdom or folly. This notion is called the principle of retributive justice and does not begin to do justice to the complexity of human decisions and relationships.

Another danger in the wisdom perspective is its tendency to avoid extremes. Wisdom is often related to moderation. This, of course, can sometimes be a virtue but also tends to weight things in favor of maintaining order in the status quo. Many of the prophets would hardly have been considered wise by the standards of Proverbs.

Fortunately, within the Wisdom literature itself some of these dangers were recognized. The clearest example is the book of Job. Job is an eloquent reflection on some of the most disturbing issues we confront in human experience: the meaning of suffering, the justice of God, the nature of our humanity. Here we can only touch briefly on the riches of this profound but disturbing and difficult book. In our context we want to stress the book of Job as a devastating protest to the notion of retributive justice.

In Job 1–2 the well-known story of the pious sufferer is told. Losing everything and suffering personally, Job nevertheless remains faithful. Unfortunately, this is the only picture of Job that many people know (symbolized by the phrase "the patience of Job"). In chapters 3–31, in dialogue with three friends, another Job appears who is anything but patient. He rages at God and at his friends, declaring the injustice of his fate. The friends respond at first with the pious orthodoxies of the wisdom perspective. Since God will reward the righteous, Job is urged to patience; God will surely adjust matters. But under the prodding of Job's anger and sarcasm, the friends soon turn the notion of retributive justice upside down. Since Job is suffering extreme loss and pain, he must therefore be guilty of sin. We the readers know, of course, that this is not true. Even God acknowledges the uprightness of Job. Although Job does not convince his friends, the book of Job forces us to acknowledge that "bad things happen to good people." Retributive justice works only in theory. In reality, material success is no measure of righteousness or wickedness. We are forced to see how often our rigid orthodoxies fail to take account of human realities. In the end of the book (chs. 38–42), God appears in a whirlwind to confront Job with the power of God as Creator and the position of Job as creature. These chapters and their meaning are greatly debated, but some observations seem reasonably clear. Job sees more clearly than his friends, but in the end he too is unwilling to part with the notion of retributive justice. He wants God to put things right—to give him back his just rewards. In confrontation with God, Job learns that retributive justice is truly not operative. Even perfect righteousness cannot lay claim on God. The Creator is radically free, and we as creatures, no matter how righteous, are dependent on God's grace and not on some system of obligating God by our righteousness. The book of Job does not answer all our questions about the difficult issues it raises, but it clears away many of the dead ends to which rigid notions of retributive justice would bring us.

TERRORS AND VISIONS

The history of the Jews in Jerusalem after the time of Ezra continued to be one of hardship. Persian rule was replaced by Greek when Alexander the Great conquered much of the known world. Following his death, Judah was controlled at times by Greek rulers in Egypt and at other times by Greek rulers in Syria. Finally, under Syrian domination, pressure began to grow for forcing all Syrian subjects, especially the Jews, to adopt Hellenistic culture (including its religion). This policy reached its height in 168 B.C. when the Syrian king Antiochus (IV) Epiphanes marched his troops into Jerusalem, desecrated the temple, and attempted to force all Jews at the point of the sword to worship Zeus. This persecution touched off the Maccabean revolt, a rebellion against Greek rule that led to a brief period of Jewish independence.

At the height of these persecutions the book of Daniel was written, to encourage the Jews in their loyalty to Yahweh and their resistance to the policies of Antiochus. Daniel belongs to a class of literature called apocalyptic (from the Greek word meaning "to uncover, reveal"), and this represents a third theological perspective that emerges in the postexilic period. Daniel (especially chs. 7–12) is the primary example of apocalyptic literature in the Old Testament, although portions of Ezekiel and Zechariah anticipate some of its features. There are several apocalyptic books in the apocrypha, and the book of Revelation in the New Testament is a fine example.

Apocalyptic literature is characterized by strange visions, bizarre symbolism, and a desire to hide its meaning from all but the faithful inner circle. Its central theme is anticipation of the end of history, when God will usher in the divine kingdom and the new age. The forces of evil will be vanquished once and for all in a final battle. In symbolic language, apocalyptic literature interprets the events of the time of persecution when it was written and then attempts to describe the events leading up to the end time and God's vindication of the faithful.

Apocalyptic books like Daniel emerge in times of persecution when the hopelessness of present events makes necessary a renewal of the vision of God's ultimate purposes for history. If one can see history moving toward God's ultimate fulfillment of the age and the vindication of the faithful, one can endure the sufferings of the present. In the book of Daniel this is made even more explicit by prefacing the apocalyptic visions of chapters 7 to 12 with stories of the pious youth Daniel and his friends remaining faithful to Yahweh against great odds in the time of the Babylonian exile (chs. 1–6).

At its best, apocalyptic reminds us of the visionary side of biblical faith, which always understands the future as God's future and therefore lives in confidence that the future holds possibilities even when crisis looms. It also reminds us of the biblical sense that history moves forward with purpose according to God's plan for the reconciliation of this broken world. For the community of faith, history does not go meaninglessly in circles. The visionaries of the Old Testament remind us of that quality of anticipation that must always mark the life of God's people and fuel our hope in the most hopeless times.

But apocalyptic also has its dangers. The apocalyptic perspective has often become so hopeless of possibilities within history that it regards all history as captured by evil. The tendency is then to give up on labor for justice and righteousness in our own time and to live only in longing for the end of time. In the period between the Old and New Testaments this led some groups, expecting and longing for the end of the age, to withdraw into communities in the desert to prepare and wait for the end time. Qumran, the community of the Dead Sea Scrolls, was one such community. Throughout Christian history, interest in the apocalyptic literature has thrived when hopelessness for the present increased. Many churches and movements in the history of the church fell victim to the temptation to give up faithful labor for the sake of God's kingdom in the present in favor of a world-denying wait for the consummation of God's kingdom that never came.

Jesus Christ Is Our Peace

The Old Testament does not come to a neat end point where all loose ends are tied up in a fitting conclusion. The book of Daniel is probably the last Old Testament book to be written. There are important and edifying books written later than this. Many of them are included in what we call the Apocrypha, but for a variety of reasons the Hebrew canon was closed after Daniel. So the Old Testament simply ends in the middle of the ongoing story of the Jews.

For the Christian church this is, of course, not the end of our scripture. Many earlier figures in the history of the church, including some influential twentieth-century theologians, have thought that there was a radical discontinuity between the Old and the New Testament. It was almost as if we had two different scriptures witnessing to two different Gods.

Fortunately, modern scholarship has taken quite a different direction. Recent studies emphasize the close and important relationship between the Old and the New Testament. Increasingly, our understanding of the New Testament must acknowledge the deep roots of the witness of the early church in the Hebrew tradition.

This allows us to see clearly that in Jesus Christ, the very center of our faith, we see, not something totally new and unheard of, but the fulfillment of all that had gone before. God in Christ is none other than the God Israel knew. The Word made flesh to dwell among us is the Word which was in the beginning with the Creator. Jesus himself declared that he had come in fulfillment of the Hebrew tradition (Matt. 5:17; Luke 4:21).

When the early church sought to interpret to the world the radical presence of God in the life, death, and resurrection of Jesus Christ, there were no better categories at hand for that witness than those already available to them in the Old Testament scripture. So they proclaimed Jesus to be the embodiment and fulfillment of all that had gone before.

Jesus is the new creation, a second Adam. He is the fulfillment of the promise given to the ancestors, the true seed of Abraham. Jesus is the one whose resurrection releases from bondage to death and brings deliverance into new life. Baptism is both a passing through the waters to new life (Exodus) and a rising from death to new life (Resurrection). Jesus is a second Moses, the giver of a new covenant. He teaches the law on the mountain (Sermon on the Mount); he appears on the Mount of Transfiguration with Moses and Elijah (the only two Old

Testament figures who ascend Mount Sinai). Jesus also fulfills the royal tradition. He is the true Messiah (anointed one), the Son of David, anointed by a prophet (John the Baptist) and proclaimer of the kingdom of God. He is Immanuel, the root from the stump of Jesse, the Prince of Peace (Isaiah 7; 9; and 11), the long-awaited one who will reign in justice and righteousness. Jesus is pictured in prophetic terms as well. He announces his ministry in Luke 4 by declaring his prophetic vocation, reading from Isaiah 61, "The Spirit of the Lord is upon me . . . to preach good news to the poor . . . release to the captives . . . sight to the blind . . . liberty to those who are oppressed." He confronts the powerful, champions the outcast and the powerless, proclaims God's word. He teaches in images drawn from ordinary life like one of the sages. He is the great high priest after the order of Melchizedek (epistle to the Hebrews), whose sacrifice makes all future sacrifices unnecessary, thus fulfilling the priestly tradition. Jesus is the Son of Man who will come again on the clouds of glory to usher in God's kingdom at the end of the age.

In short, without the witness of the Old Testament, we frequently would have little idea of what the early church was saying about Jesus in the New Testament. If Jesus Christ is the flower of our faith, the Old Testament witnesses we have described in these chapters are its roots.

We can close by calling on the great Hebrew symbol of *shalom* (wholeness, peace) for a concluding witness to the unity of our biblical faith. God's intention for the world in creation was *shalom*. In a broken and sinful world, God entered into covenant with Israel, and the goal of covenant community was *shalom*. Now Jesus Christ is our peace *(shalom);* he "has broken down the dividing wall of hostility . . . reconciled us both to God in one body through the cross, thereby bringing hostility to an end . . . and preached peace to you who were far off and peace to those who were near" (Eph. 2:14, 16–17). May *shalom* ever be the vision we claim, even as it claims us.

QUESTIONS
FOR DISCUSSION
* * *

CHAPTER 1: IN THE IMAGE OF GOD

1. Is the Bible an important resource for you and your congregation in making decisions about Christian life in the world? Think of ways in which you see this happening or ways in which you would like to see it happening.
2. Is the Old Testament as important for you as the New Testament? If not, why do you think this is so?
3. Have you gained new insights into the Old Testament understanding of creation from reading this chapter? Identify ideas that seem important to you in the Old Testament witness to God as Creator and in the purpose of humanity in the creation.
4. Is the brokenness described for creation in Genesis 3 something that you experience as a reality in our world? Can you describe some instances of this?

CHAPTER 2: FROM PROMISE TO DELIVERANCE

1. To be a sojourner is to live out of trust in God rather than trusting only in those things we control. Are there places in your life or your congregation where you experience this sense of trust? Are there areas

where you would like to become more trusting of God?

2. What Israel learned of the God who saves in the exodus became central to its faith. Do the things you have learned in this chapter on the meaning of the exodus event still seem central to our faith? What for you are the most important new insights into the exodus experience?

3. Is the exodus pattern of faith diagrammed on p. 46 one which you have experienced? How does this pattern help us to understand the meaning of salvation?

CHAPTER 3: YOU SHALL BE MY PEOPLE

1. Covenant community means life related to God as an alternative community in the world. In what ways have you seen the church acting in ways different from its surrounding culture? Are there ways in which you would like to see the church risk more as an alternative community?

2. In this chapter we speak of the freedom, vulnerability, and fidelity of God. Are these new ways of thinking about God for you? Can you identify insights here that are helpful in thinking about your relationship with God? About the church's relationship with God?

3. In what ways have you thought before about covenant faith as having implications for our political and economic life? Do Israel's struggles for faithfulness in these realms give you helpful insights for the church's witness in our own political and economic life?

CHAPTER 4: LIKE THE OTHER NATIONS

1. Kingship in Israel brought a challenge to covenant community. We no longer have kings, but in what ways do you see the same challenges presented to us as covenant people (*a*) through the domestication of God? (*b*) through an economics of privilege? (*c*) through a politics of oppression?
2. How does the church carry on the prophetic witness in our time? Do you see persons acting to champion the covenant concerns we discussed in the last chapter? Do you see ways in which congregations or larger church bodies can act prophetically?

CHAPTER 5: BY THE WATERS OF BABYLON

1. Have you or someone you know experienced occasions of feeling abandoned by God? If possible, share some of these moments and their emotions.
2. After reading this chapter, how do you think the Israelite experience of exile might relate to our own experience of the contemporary world? Are there ways in which you see the possibility for upheaval and confusion in our cultural, political, economic, and religious life?
3. In this chapter we discuss five forms of hope in the Old Testament witness. Which of these seem most meaningful to your own experience of times when hope was needed? Were any of these ways of thinking about hope new to you? In what ways does this broader biblical picture help you to be hopeful in our present world?
4. Jesus Christ fulfills the Old Testament calling to be

the servant of the Lord and calls us to be a servant church. When the world looks at the church, does it see a servant community? In what ways could we more fully embody the biblical call to servanthood?

CHAPTER 6: SAGES, VISIONARIES, AND POETS

1. In the period after exile, Israel entered a time in which several viewpoints on faith struggled for attention. In what ways do the following perspectives give you new insights or warn of dangers to our faith?
   a. The reforms of Ezra and Nehemiah
   b. The wisdom tradition
   c. Apocalyptic literature (Daniel)
2. List the categories from the Old Testament used by the New Testament writers in their proclamation about Jesus. What difference does this make for you in understanding the relationship of the Old Testament to the New Testament? (You may wish to use a concordance to look up some of the New Testament uses of these Old Testament categories in describing Jesus. This may help in seeing more fully the importance of the Old Testament in the New Testament witness to Jesus.)
3. Now that you have finished the book, how has your attitude toward the Old Testament changed? Share what for you have been the most important new insights into this portion of our scripture. Identify an area in which you might wish to do further study.

SUGGESTIONS
FOR FURTHER READING
* * *

CHAPTER 1: IN THE IMAGE OF GOD

Bruce C. Birch and Larry L. Rasmussen, *The Predicament of the Prosperous; Biblical Perspectives on Current Issues* (Westminster Press, 1978), ch. 5.

Walter Brueggemann, *Genesis; Interpretation Commentaries* (John Knox Press, 1982).

Gerhard von Rad, *Genesis, A Commentary;* Old Testament Library (Westminster Press, 1973; rev. ed.).

Phyllis Trible, *God and the Rhetoric of Sexuality* (Fortress Press, 1978), ch. 4.

CHAPTER 2: FROM PROMISE TO DELIVERANCE

Walter Brueggemann, *Praying the Psalms* (St. Mary's Press, 1982).

Brevard Childs, *The Book of Exodus; A Critical, Theological Commentary;* Old Testament Library (Westminster Press, 1974).

Norman K. Gottwald, ed., *The Bible and Liberation: Politics and Social Hermeneutics* (Orbis Press, 1983).

Arthur Waskow, *Godwrestling* (Schocken Books, 1978).

CHAPTER 3: YOU SHALL BE MY PEOPLE

Bruce C. Birch, "The Covenant at Sinai: Response to God's Freedom," in *Social Themes of the Christian Year,* ed. by Dieter T. Hessel (Geneva Press, 1983).

Walter Brueggemann, *The Prophetic Imagination* (Fortress Press, 1978).

Walter Harrelson, *The Ten Commandments and Human Rights* (Fortress Press, 1980).

Delbert Hillers, *Covenant: The History of a Biblical Idea* (Johns Hopkins Press, 1969).

Chapter 4: Like the Other Nations

Bernhard Anderson, *The Eighth Century Prophets: Amos, Hosea, Isaiah, Micah;* Proclamation Commentaries (Fortress Press, 1978).

Walter Brueggemann, *The Land: Place as a Gift, Promise, and Challenge in Biblical Faith* (Fortress Press, 1977).

———, *The Prophetic Imagination* (Fortress Press, 1978).

James D. Newsome, Jr., *The Hebrew Prophets* (John Knox Press, 1984).

H. W. Wolff, *Confrontations with Prophets* (Fortress Press, 1983).

Chapter 5: By the Waters of Babylon

Bruce C. Birch, *Singing the Lord's Song: A Study of Isaiah 40–55* (Service Center, Women's Division of the General Board of Global Ministries of the United Methodist Church, 1981).

——— and Larry L. Rasmussen, *The Predicament of the Prosperous;* Biblical Perspectives on Current Issues (Westminster Press, 1978), ch. 6.

Ralph W. Klein, *Israel in Exile: A Theological Interpretation* (Fortress Press, 1979).

James Luther Mays, *Ezekiel, Second Isaiah;* Proclamation Commentaries (Fortress Press, 1978).

Chapter 6: Sages, Visionaries, and Poets

Walter Brueggemann, *In Man We Trust: The Neglected Side of Biblical Faith* (John Knox Press, 1972).

James L. Crenshaw, *Old Testament Wisdom: An Introduction* (John Knox Press, 1981).

H. L. Ellison, *From Babylon to Bethlehem* (John Knox Press, 1979).

D. S. Russell, *Apocalyptic: Ancient and Modern* (Fortress Press, 1978).

W. Sibley Towner, *Daniel;* Interpretation Commentaries (John Knox Press, 1983).

Bruce Vawter, *Job and Jonah: Questioning the Hidden God* (Paulist Press, 1983).